GOOD THINGS FOR BABIES

ALSO BY SANDY JONES

Learning for Little Kids

GOOD THINGS FOR BABIES

Sandy Jones

Line drawings by Sally L. Wright

Second Edition, Revised

HOUGHTON MIFFLIN COMPANY BOSTON 1980

Library of Congress Cataloging in Publication Data

Jones, Sandy.
☐ Good things for babies.

☐ Includes bibliographies and index.
☐ 1. Infants--Care and hygiene. 2. Infants'
supplies--Catalogs. I. Title.
RJ61.J73 1980   649'.122'028   79-29726
ISBN 0-395-29197-6
ISBN 0-395-29198-4 pbk.

Printed in the United States of America

Q 10 9 8 7 6 5 4 3 2 1

To the breastfeeding mother,
who gives her baby the most precious gift of all — herself.

Contents

Introduction

Babies can't protect their own rights to health and safety, but we, as parents, can, by being constantly vigilant of our babies and by selecting products for them carefully. America the bountiful is churning out billions of products annually. And thousands of babies are being hurt by many of them. Unfortunately, most of the things being manufactured aren't designed for babies at all! They're designed for the comfort and convenience of adults. Massive advertising campaigns convince us that babies need useless, expensive, and sometimes harmful products. Few companies have studied the measurements of infants, or how babies develop, or what they truly need as they grow.

Good Things for Babies has been written to guide you, the new parent, in finding well-designed products and good information to help you during your first two years with Baby. The products in this book have been chosen because they are truly useful to parents and babies. Each has been selected because it offers maximum safety, convenience, and helpfulness. In some cases, the best products haven't been made yet — for instance, cribs that are free from bruising bars, or strollers that conform comfortably to babies' physical dimensions. Some of the products are really expensive, but they will show you what to look for when shopping and demonstrate what could be made at competitive prices if parents really wanted these products. Incidentally, no company has influenced me or paid me to include a product in the book. I've chosen independently, using my knowledge of infant development, my extensive studies of infant-injury reports, and interviews with parents of babies.

Good Things for Babies was born half a year after our wiry little Marcie. After watching the babies in a mother-infant group I participated in, I became aware of how all babies seem to grow in unison and in harmony with inner laws of sequence. As we, the mothers, sat together each week to share our problems and experiences, I began to see the real need we had for good, practical advice on how to choose products. It's not that we had a lot of money to spend on our babies. We didn't. That's why we had to choose wisely — we couldn't afford to buy shoddy or unsafe things. And thus I started the exciting hunt — somewhat like searching for a needle in a haystack — for the best in design for babies. The search has led me around the world by mail. I was always looking for products that had a special correctness — a "fit" that seemed just right, according to what I know about babies and their development.

I also sought to find out, through medical reports in pediatric journals, how babies have been hurt by products. With the help of the National Safety Council, the International Organization of Consumer's Unions, and the U.S. Consumer Product Safety Commission, I've been able to pinpoint what bad products are doing to babies.

Now it is time for a second edition. I am amazed at how quickly products have diversified and improved — particularly car seats, baby toys, and strollers. I think parents are becoming much more aware as consumers now, as witnessed by the thousands of complaints about infant products on file at the U.S. Consumer Product Safety Commission offices. New regulations are now in effect, or in the offing, for car seats, rattles, and small objects that are often aspirated by babies. Voluntary safety standards for highchairs and playpens have been adopted by members of the Juvenile Products Manufacturers Association; other product categories are now in the process of being established.

Last year I interviewed over 200 mothers and fathers of babies to find out their experiences with "things for babies." Their two major complaints were that products were not durable and that they hurt babies because of poor design.

If ever there was a time for "parent power" it is now. Parents must lead the way to bring about change in safety standards for babies and young children. The regulation of small rattles, for example, resulted from the work of a young mother whose infant daughter suffocated on a small rattle shaped like a telephone receiver. Many parents are expressing their consumer concerns through groups like Action for Child Transportation Safety and Parents Action Coalition for Toys.

I thank the readers of the last edition who took time to write me about their product concerns. As a result of this help, several potentially hazardous products have been removed from the book. Other products, though well designed, have been discontinued by manufacturers, while over 100 new items have been added.

If you find a product in the book that isn't a good thing for a baby, please write me in care of Houghton Mifflin and tell me why. Also, let me know about any good products that I did not turn up in my search. You can help me to make the next edition even better and more helpful to parents!

The pronouns *he* and *she* have been used in alternating chapters to give equal recognition to babies of both sexes.

I wish to express my gratitude to the many mothers who have shared with me their findings about the things that they have bought. Thanks, too, to the manufacturers of the products, who have been very gracious in providing the necessary pictures and information for the book. Special thanks go to Marcie for waiting and waiting for me to finish the book.

As I have tried to say throughout the book, love is the first and foremost thing that babies need. No product can replace the tender caressing and care of a loving parent. And no safety device can protect like a continually vigilant mom and dad.

Sandy Jones

GOOD THINGS
FOR BABIES

Basics

Babies are physical beings — they depend almost wholly on your body to tell them that they are loved. They thrive on gentle holding, caressing, rocking, and all kinds of touching — even toe nibbling! It's best, during the first months, to slow your movements down, handling your baby firmly and deliberately so that he can feel secure in your arms. Your baby also needs your voice and words to assure him that you are there and that you will care for him. During this time the foundations of trust in life and people are being formed. So don't let your baby cry for an extended period of time, since for him, crying is always a sign of discomfort and becomes more and more desperate when it's ignored. Instead, try to find the cause of his crying — perhaps he wants to change positions, to nurse, simply to be held and reassured by you. Young babies are hungry every hour and a half to two hours; it's much too early to try to schedule them into adult ideas of what babies are supposed to do.

For the first months and even the first year of Baby's life, forget about housework except the basics. Relax, put your feet up when you can, and hold and play with your baby. The luxury of his sweet softness and the special pride of being a new mother are yours to enjoy for such a short time! Be careful to get the rest you need, sleeping when he does, day and night, if you need to. Nothing can undermine your confidence as a new mother more than exhaustion and worry over not having the house just so.

Most of all, don't be afraid that you might "spoil" your baby by picking him up when he needs you or by giving in when he seems to want to be held or is hungry. Careful scientific studies conducted by Dr. Mary Ainsworth and her associates at Johns Hopkins University have shown that babies who are left to cry during their first months of life cry more during subsequent months than those whose needs are met quickly and sensitively. The popular idea that "giving in" to babies by responding too readily to their cries makes them spoiled has been proven to be wrong. On the contrary, babies who are given long, loving holding and answered quickly develop into independent, self-sufficient children much earlier. It's the babies who are treated in a rigid, insensitive way and expected to conform to adult schedules prematurely that later act spoiled — they're more likely to be clinging, quick to cry, and demanding of attention.

If you find yourself getting blue during that difficult first year, remind yourself: *Yes*, baby will finally sleep through the night! *Yes*, I will get my energy back in time and begin to feel like my old self again! *Yes*, things will get easier for me after the first year, when the baby becomes more independent!

If you have a fussy, colicky baby, you need more time out than the mom with a placid, content baby does. Sometimes a walk in the fresh air, with or without Baby, a nice hot shower, or a brief nap will be enough to recharge your batteries so that you can deal with him again.

Several holding techniques may help to ease Baby's gas pains. Try holding him prone while you're standing, one arm supporting his chest, the other between his legs and supporting his belly. Gently massage his belly with your hand. Or you might try sitting him almost erect in an infant seat so that he's facing a lamp or some other bright light. Some mothers of colicky babies have really gotten good results rocking Baby in an automatic baby swing. (You might be able to find an inexpensive used one.) Babies almost uniformly outgrow colic after the first three months, so hang in there — things will soon be better!

In the second half of Baby's first year, he begins to

turn over, sit by himself, crawl, creep and then walk. He begins to discover that there are other people in the world besides himself, and he loves to explore the world of objects. He learns about his world by mouthing, touching, and handling. This natural drive to explore shouldn't be inhibited by confining him in a crib or playpen. He should be free to move about the house, and outdoors, too, always in close touch with you, his "home base." You must be careful to baby-proof your house (see "Safety and Poison Prevention," pp. 77–85), and keep a constant eye on him to see that he doesn't hurt himself.

Forget about trying to instill discipline at this age. It's hopeless! You can slap his hand for pulling down an ashtray and two minutes later he'll pull it down again. He's just too young yet to be able to follow commands. It's a harassing time for parents, with a lot of falls and crying for baby, but it paves the way to a graceful, well-coordinated toddlerhood.

Most first-time parents — and grandparents, too, for that matter — expect too much of a baby too soon. They think he should be sleeping through the night, when he still seems to need night feeding. They want him to be independent, when he still needs closeness and reassurance very much. They want him to be disciplined, when he's still too young to understand such things, and toilet-trained before he has sufficient control of his body. Babies need to be accepted just as they are, with a generous amount of physical contact, comforting, and play. That takes a lot of flexibility and energy on your part, but it pays off in the long run, making a happier, more secure child.

A NOTE ABOUT "ADVICE" BOOKS

The following books and magazines have been selected because they're practical and genuinely helpful regarding day-to-day life with baby. Bookstores and libraries offer hundreds of advice books to parents. Every publisher wants to cash in on the "new parent market" by offering one more noted pediatrician advising parents what to do with their babies and children. Most of the advice is bland. What one authority sets forth as an ultimatum of baby care, another "expert" will reverse. Few child-care authorities take into account the needs of mothers and fathers on a daily basis — in fact, in most books dealing with babies, the parents exist only in the shadows, whereas the infant is presented as a "case" separate from his family.

The books in the following lists have been chosen because they help mothers and fathers with everyday

things in a human, sensitive way. They're not best sellers and probably never will be — but they're good and will prove worthwhile investments.

BOOKS FOR TELLING YOUR BABY'S STORY

Baby's Journal
Metropolitan Museum of Art
Dist. by Charles Scribner's Sons, 597 Fifth Ave., NYC 10017 ($8.95)
A charming book brought alive from the 1900s with classic illustrations of mother and baby throughout. Ample space is provided for recording ceremonies, gifts, games, and words of wisdom. An excellent shower gift!

Especially for You
La Leche League International, 9616 Minneapolis Ave., Franklin Park, IL 60131 ($11.95)
A breastfed baby's record book, which includes a place for both mother and father to describe labor and delivery, a page to tell about Baby's first nursing, and a place to record Baby's nursing habits and preferences. Poetry written by mothers is sprinkled throughout.

The Nubian Baby Book:
Our Baby's First Seven Years
Clarence L. Holte, Ed.
Nubian Press, 507 Fifth Ave., NYC 10017 ($8.00)
A baby book for black babies and parents. Includes African proverbs, Afro-American poetry, and advice on environmental hazards as well as spaces for record keeping. Illustrations of black babies and children at play.

Our Baby's Early Years
Lenora Moragne and Rudolph Moragne
Len Champs Publishers, P.O. Box 23432, Washington, DC 20024 ($4.45)
A concise little record book for black parents written by a black physician in cooperation with a nutrition expert. Financial advice and suggestions regarding immunization and nutrition are included, as well as spaces for recording Baby's vital information.

Our Baby's First Seven Years
Mothers' Aid of the Chicago Lying-in Hospital, MH 445, 5841 Maryland Ave., Chicago, IL 60637 ($5.00 + 50¢ handling)
A superb baby-record book. Includes up-to-date information on the stages of development of babies, and spaces for recording important information and medical data. A guidance book as well as a record book, it is published under the auspices of the University of Chicago Lying-In Hospital, where its sales help to support research.

Watch Me Grow
Vicki Lansky and Bruce Lansky
Meadowbrook Press, 16648 Meadowbrook Ln., Wayzata, MN 55391 ($8.00 + $1.00 postage and handling)
This spiral-bound hardback album allows for great flexibility in what you record about the significance of your baby's and child's life. It resembles an open-ended calendar. Space is provided for pictures and for recording early events. There is an envelope inside the back cover for storing birthday cards and other mementos.

PERIODICALS AND BOOK CLUBS

Children Today
Superintendent of Documents, U.S. Government Printing Office, Washington, DC 20402 ($6.10 per year)
Published by the Children's Bureau of the U.S. Department of Health, Education and Welfare, this inexpensive magazine, with its reviews of new books and descriptions of new programs for babies and young children, will help keep you up-to-date. Particularly of interest to parents involved in day care.

Growing Child
22 N. Second St., Lafayette, IN 47902 ($7.95 per year)
When you subscribe to *Growing Child*, you will receive a newsletter each month of your baby's first year filled with information about the skills your baby is developing, playthings and activities suited to his level, and practical child-care tips. An excellent investment! Send Baby's name, birth date, and parents' names. Newsletters go up to four years of age.

Parents Magazine
52 Vanderbilt Ave., NYC 10017 ($7.95 per year)
Consistently sound articles on baby care as well as advice on rearing older children. Book reviews, recipes, and articles on decorating, are all included. Articles are relatively free from the influence of advertisers.

Practical Parenting
15235 Minnetonka Blvd., Minnetonka, MN 55343 ($5.00/ 6 issues)
A bimonthly newsletter by and for parents. It contains updates on nutrition and medicine, practical hints for coping with toddlers and young children, and numerous handy suggestions sent in by parents.

Young Parents Book Club
Stamford, CT 06904
This book club carries most of the major books on childcare at a discount. The club magazine is mailed every four weeks. The main selection is mailed automatically, unless the club is notified. Members are required to make four selections beyond the initial special offer. Write for information.

The following magazines are most useful for new and expectant mothers. Usually each issue features several helpful articles on baby and child care. Some of these magazines are more heavily slanted toward advertising and attempt to influence mothers to buy products.

American Baby
575 Lexington Ave., NYC 10022

Baby Talk
66 East 34 St., NYC 10016

Mothers' Manual
P.O. Box 243, Franklin Lakes, NJ 07417

GENERAL PARENTING GUIDES

Although many of these books deal with specific problems encountered by parents, their main thrust is in providing a "philosophy" of parenting — a way of approaching the whole experience of having a baby and rearing a child.

Birth Without Violence
Frederick Leboyer
Alfred A. Knopf, 201 E. 50th St., NYC 10022 ($8.95)
A revolutionary, compassionate book that details Dr. Leboyer's simple but effective methods for handling newborn babies to give them a feeling of security. Recommended reading for all parents-in-waiting!

The First Five Years
Dr. Virginia E. Pomeranz and Dodi Schultz
Dell Publishing Co., 1 Dag Hammarskjöld Plaza, 245 E. 47th St., NYC 10017 ($1.75, paperback)
Drawing on her twenty years' experience as a pediatrician, Dr. Pomeranz has written an extremely practical, relaxed book about child care. She explains: "If you react naturally in dealing with your child, you will at least be consistent. Should you make any mistakes, they will tend to be the same ones time after time; thus, the child will not be confused by wide discrepancies in your reactions to him." Very readable, and soothing to a new parent.

Enjoy Your Child — Ages 1, 2, and 3
James L. Hymes, Jr.
Public Affairs Pamphlet No. 141, Public Affairs Committee, Inc., 381 Park Ave. S., NYC 10016 (35¢)
A brochure written by an authority in the field of early childhood education that stresses a relaxed, easy-going approach to dealing with the everyday problems of child rearing. Suggests ways truly to *enjoy* your child.

Growing with Children
Joseph L. Braga and Laurie D. Braga
Prentice-Hall, Englewood Cliffs, NJ 07632
($2.95, paperback)
The authors draw upon excerpts from the writings of
noted authorities in child development to present a
sensitive explanation of what parents can provide for
the emotional growth of their babies and children.

How to Parent
Dr. Fitzhugh Dodson
New American Library, 1301 Ave. of the Americas, NYC
10019 ($2.25, paperback)
Dr. Dodson, a psychologist, deals not only with parents'
feelings about the experience of baby and child rearing,
but also with the child's needs and his self-concept.
A practical source book that includes lists of suggested
books for parents, and toys, books, and music for
babies and children.

The Magic Years: Understanding and Handling the Problems of Early Childhood
Selma H. Fraiberg
Charles Scribner's Sons, 597 Fifth Ave., NYC 10017
($2.95, paperback)
A sensitive guide to understanding why babies and
toddlers act the way they do. You'll particularly enjoy
Fraiberg's interpretation of toddlerhood and the "terri-
ble twos" from the child's standpoint, and her clarifi-
cation of the reasons older babies have sleeping
problems.

Maternal-Infant Bonding
Marshall H. Klaus and John H. Kennell
C. V. Mosby Co., 2700 E. Bates Ave., Denver, CO 80210
($7.50, paperback)
Physicians describe their important discoveries about
the bonding of mothers to their babies and the profound effects of separation of mother and baby during
the hours after birth. The discussion on the loss of a
baby is particularly helpful for grieving parents.

Oneness and Separateness: From Infant to Individual
Louise J. Kaplan
Simon & Schuster, 1230 Ave. of the Americas, NYC 10020
($9.95)
With powerful, almost poetic language, Kaplan takes
us into the world of feelings, where rage and love
coexist in the relationship between mother and baby.
The crucial steps in a baby's development into a separate person are articulated. Heavy reading, but with
the potential for profound personal meaning.

Touching: The Human Significance of the Skin
Ashley Montague
Harper & Row, Publishers, 10 E. 53rd St., NYC 10022
($4.95, paperback)
A superb book of caregiving that draws from many
fields to stress the importance of handling, breastfeeding, caressing, and rocking babies. Excellent reading
for expectant parents!

Your First Months with Your First Baby
Alicerose Barman
Public Affairs Pamphlet No. 478, Public Affairs
Committee, Inc., 381 Park Ave. S., NYC 10016
(25¢)
A discussion of how a new parent's life-style changes,
how babies differ temperamentally, and how you, as a
new parent, can provide optimum conditions for your
baby's growth.

BABY-CARE AND MEDICAL ADVICE BOOKS

Baby and Child Care
Dr. Benjamin Spock
Pocket Books, 630 Fifth Ave., NYC 10020
($1.95)
A 600-page volume that discusses *everything!* Teething,
colds, breastfeeding, toilet training — whatever you
can think of, you will find in the index. You may want
to try raising your baby without Spock — but the book
will somehow manage to sneak home hidden in a bag
of groceries.

Child Care
ROCOM, Division of Hoffmann-LaRoche, Inc., Dept. JE,
Nutley, NJ 07110
($5.95 + 85¢ shipping)
An easy-to-read health-care manual that answers many
questions new parents have about colic, diaper rash,
reactions to immunizations, sore throats, and other ail-
ments. Profusely illustrated with photographs of
babies and children and equipped with a helpful
checklist of information that you should have ready for
the doctor when you call about an illness.

Childhood Illness: A Common Sense Approach
Jack G. Shiller, M.D.
Stein & Day Publishers, 7 E. 48th St., NYC 10017
($2.45, paperback)
A fantastic little volume that will help you to discern
what illnesses you can treat by yourself at home and
when you should seek medical help. It also tells you
how to take care of your sick child. Chapters are
arranged according to symptoms and are written in
easy-to-understand terms. The book includes an explanation of medical terms, immunization schedules,
growth charts, and even a listing of drugs you can buy
without a prescription for treating colds, coughs, diaper rash, etc.

The Family Book of Child Care
Niles Newton
Harper & Row, Publishers, 10 E. 53rd St., NYC 10022
($12.95)
An excellent child-care book that is truly helpful! It's
written by an experienced mother who is also a scien-
tist. The advice is practical, down-to-earth, and well
researched. A very good investment and a thoughtful
shower gift.

Infant Care

Superintendent of Documents, U.S. Government Printing Office, Washington, DC 20402 ($1.00)
An inexpensive, basic baby-care manual from the Children's Bureau of the U.S. Department of Health, Education and Welfare. It discusses how babies differ and lists developmental skills from month to month. Includes suggestions for toys and safety advice.

The Well Baby Book

Mike Samuels, M.D., and Nancy Samuels
Simon & Schuster, 1230 Ave. of the Americas, NYC 10020 ($8.95, paperback)
A giant 400-page paperback volume with advice on everything from the psychological development of babies and toddlers to dealing with everyday medical problems. This book will give you more than you ever thought you could find in print!

Your Baby and Child

Penelope Leach
Alfred A. Knopf, 201 E. 50th St., NYC 10028 ($15.95)
A super encyclopedia for the first five years with your child. It includes first aid measures, a growth chart, breast care and milk expression, feeding suggestions, and excellent photos and illustrations.

Your Child and You: A Pediatrician Talks to New Mothers

David T. Hellyer, M.D.
Delacorte Press, Dell Publishing Co., 1 Dag Hammarskjöld Plaza, 245 E. 47th St., NYC 10017
(No longer in print, but available at most libraries.)
Dr. Hellyer's book is written primarily for the first-time mother. The book traces Baby's development through each month of the first year and describes what to expect in the next four years. The author is sensitive to the questions that most often plague a new mother — for example, what to do about problems with Baby's sleeping, feeding, and teething.

FREE OR INEXPENSIVE HEALTH BROCHURES

Atopic Eczema or Atopic Dermatitis

(OP-379, 30¢) Order Department, American Medical Association, 535 N. Dearborn St., Chicago, IL 60610

Doctor, Is My Baby Deaf?

Alexander Graham Bell Association for the Deaf, 3417 Volta Pl., N.W., Washington, DC 20007 (Free; send stamped, self-addressed envelope)
Gives danger signals and steps to take if hearing impairment is suspected.

Immunization

(OP-19, 20¢) Order Department, American Medical Association, 535 N. Dearborn St., Chicago, IL 60610

Memo to Parents about Immunization

Metropolitan Life Insurance Co., 1 Madison Ave., NYC 10010 (Free)

Vascular Birthmarks and Your Child

(OP-89, 15¢) Order Department, American Medical Association, 535 N. Dearborn St., Chicago, IL 60610

Your Baby's Eyes

American Optometric Association, 7000 Chippewa St., St. Louis, MO 63119 (Free; send stamped self-addressed envelope)

GUIDES TO INFANT DEVELOPMENT

These guides take you month-by-month through the growth and development of a baby, telling you what to look for in the months ahead.

The First Twelve Months of Life

Frank Caplan, Ed.
Grosset & Dunlap, 51 Madison Ave., NYC 10010 ($5.95, paperback)
This best seller on parenthood offers a month-by-month description of baby development. The strength of the book is its hundreds of photographs of babies at various ages and stages.

Guide to the Care of Infants in Groups

Sally Provence, M.D.
Child Welfare League of America, Inc., 67 Irving Pl., NYC 10003 ($3.00, paperback)
A superbly detailed statement of how babies develop month by month. Includes a developmental landmarks chart outlining body mastery, speech, hand skills, and growth through the first two years.

Infants and Mothers: Differences in Development

T. Berry Brazelton, M.D.
Dell Publishing Co., 1 Dag Hammarskjöld Plaza, 245 E. 47th St., NYC 10017 ($6.95, paperback)
Dr. Brazelton traces the growth and skills of three babies — quiet, average, and active — showing how each differs even in the early months. A good child-care advice book as well.

Toddlers and Parents

T. Berry Brazelton, M.D.
Delacorte Press, Dell Publishing Co., 1 Dag Hammarskjöld Plaza, 245 E. 47th St., NYC 10017 ($10.00)
Dr. Brazelton uses examples of typical toddlers and their behavior to discuss toddler relationships with peers and parents. He discusses sleeping problems, rebellious behavior, and other hurdles for parents of one- to three-year-olds.

"What to Expect of a Baby from One to Twelve Months"
Service Editor, Baby Talk *Magazine, 66 E. 34th St., NYC 10016 (40¢ + 35¢ service charge)*
A *Baby Talk* reprint co-authored by *Baby Talk* and the Department of Pediatrics, School of Medicine, Duke University. Highlights of each month of growth; many photographs.

BOOKS TO GUIDE YOU IN FOSTERING BABY'S DEVELOPMENT

The Baby Exercise Book for the First Fifteen Months
Dr. Janine Lévy
Random House, 201 E. 50th St., NYC 10022 ($3.95, paperback)
A French specialist in infant physical development guides you in exercises for your baby specifically designed to aid in balance and coordination. Suggests easy-to-use equipment.

Getting Your Baby Ready to Talk
John Tracy Clinic, 806 W. Adams Blvd., Los Angeles, CA 90007 ($4.00 postpaid, paperback)
A large mimeographed handbook of day-to-day ways to encourage Baby's speech through play activities. It's sectioned into enjoyable "lessons" that begin at birth and go through two years of age. Well worth the money!

How to Teach Your Baby to Swim
Claire Timmermans
Stein & Day, Scarborough House, Briarcliff Manor, NY 10510 ($2.95, paperback)
The emphasis in Timmermans' book is on the safety of the baby and his security in the water. Numerous photographs of babies demonstrate basic skills for keeping afloat. This is a sensitively written, practical book based on the author's own experience as a mother, swimmer, and instructor.

Suzy Prudden's Creative Fitness for Baby and Child
Suzy Prudden and Jeffrey Sussman
William Morrow & Co., 105 Madison Ave., NYC 10016 ($6.95)
A series of exercises for babies and children, with excellent photographs and creative ideas for developing your own exercise program.

Teaching an Infant to Swim
Virginia Hunt Newman
Harcourt Brace Jovanovich, 757 Third Ave., NYC 10021 ($2.45, paperback)
A well-known swimming instructor explains fully and clearly her method for teaching water safety to infants eight months of age and older.

Teach Your Child to Talk
Parent Handbook, CEBCO/Standard Publishing Co., 104 Fifth Ave., NYC 10011 ($1.75, paperback)
An excellent handbook for parents that divides growth in communication by age and suggests practical everyday activities to enhance communication development. Inexpensive pamphlets and toys are suggested.

Total Baby Development
Jaroslav Koch
Pocket Books, 1230 Ave. of the Americas, NYC 10020 ($3.95, paperback)
An internationally respected psychologist at the Institute for the Care of Mother and Child in Prague has designed 122 simple, pleasant exercises to enhance Baby's development from 30 days to one year of age.

FOR BABIES WITH PHYSICAL PROBLEMS

Diana L. Brown, in *Developmental Handicaps in Babies and Young Children* (see p. 7), reports that each year in the United States more than 200,000 babies are born with a handicap, defect, or deformity. Some problems show up at birth; others are not noticed until later. It's important that you, as a parent, be informed about what progress to expect from your baby and that you report to your doctor any concerns you might have about his development.

The following nonprofit organizations have literature that may prove helpful to you. Write for their publications listings:

ALEXANDER GRAHAM BELL ASSOCIATION FOR THE DEAF
3417 Volta Pl., N.W., Washington, DC 20007

ALLERGY FOUNDATION OF AMERICA
801 Second Ave., NYC 10017

AMERICAN ASSOCIATION ON MENTAL DEFICIENCIES
520 Connecticut Ave., N.W., Washington, DC 20009

AMERICAN DIABETES ASSOCIATION
18 E. 48th St., NYC 10017

AMERICAN FOUNDATION FOR THE BLIND
15 W. 16th St., NYC 10011

AMERICAN HEART ASSOCIATION
7320 Greenville Ave., Dallas, TX 75231

AMERICAN SPEECH AND HEARING ASSOCIATION
9030 Old Georgetown Rd., Washington, DC 20014

ARTHRITIS FOUNDATION
1212 Ave. of the Americas, NYC 10036

ASSOCIATION FOR CHILDREN WITH LEARNING
DISABILITIES
4156 Library Rd. Pittsburgh, PA 15234

CHILDREN'S BUREAU
*U.S. Dept. of Health, Education and Welfare,
P.O. Box 1182, Washington, DC 20013*
Publishes booklets about children with mental or
physical handicaps.

COUNCIL FOR EXCEPTIONAL CHILDREN
1920 Association Dr., Reston, VA 22091

CYSTIC FIBROSIS FOUNDATION
3379 Peachtree Rd., N.E., Atlanta, GA 30326

DEAFNESS RESEARCH FOUNDATION
366 Madison Ave., NYC 10017

EPILEPSY FOUNDATION OF AMERICA
1828 L St., N.W., Washington, DC 20036

MUSCULAR DYSTROPHY ASSOCIATIONS OF
AMERICA
1790 Broadway, NYC 10019

NATIONAL ASSOCIATION FOR RETARDED
CITIZENS
2709 Ave. E, East Arlington, TX 76011

NATIONAL CYSTIC FIBROSIS RESEARCH
FOUNDATION
202 E. 44th St., NYC 10017

NATIONAL EASTER SEAL SOCIETY FOR CRIPPLED
CHILDREN AND ADULTS
2023 W. Ogden Ave., Chicago, IL 60612
Publishes brochures covering a broad range of physical
disabilities, including cleft palate, and learning
disabilities.

NATIONAL FOUNDATION — MARCH OF DIMES
1275 Mamaroneck Ave., White Plains, NY 10605
Deals with birth defects, their prevention and
treatment.

NATIONAL HEMOPHILIA FOUNDATION
25 W. 39th St., NYC 10018

NATIONAL KIDNEY FOUNDATION
315 Park Ave. S., NYC 10010

NATIONAL SOCIETY FOR AUTISTIC CHILDREN
169 Tampa Ave., Albany, NY 12208

NATIONAL SOCIETY FOR THE PREVENTION
OF BLINDNESS
79 Madison Ave., NYC 10016

NATIONAL SUDDEN INFANT DEATH SYNDROME
FOUNDATION
301 S. Michigan Ave., Chicago, IL 60604

OSTEOGENESIS IMPERFECTA FOUNDATION
*% Mr. C. C. Neely, 1231 May Court, Burlington, NC
27215*

UNITED CEREBRAL PALSY ASSOCIATIONS, INC.
66 E. 34th St., NYC 10016

The following books have proved helpful to parents of
handicapped or retarded babies and young children:

**Developmental Handicaps in Babies and Young
Children: A Guide for Parents**
Diana L. Brown
*Charles C. Thomas, Publisher, 301–27 E. Lawrence Ave.,
Springfield, IL 62717 ($5.75)*
An excellent book for parents who suspect that something may be wrong with their baby, perhaps because
he is slow in developing or seems different from other
babies. The book clearly defines different disabilities
and gives parents specific suggestions as to where to
go for help.

**Handling the Young Cerebral Palsied Child
at Home**
Nancie R. Finnie
*E. P. Dutton & Co., 2 Park Ave., NYC 10016
($4.95, paperback)*
This superb handbook, covering handling techniques,
specialized equipment, and developmental guides, will
prove useful to parents of spastic and athetoid children. Describes methods of carrying, toilet training,
and teaching self-dressing and feeding, with many do-
it-yourself ideas.

**What to Do about Your Brain-Injured Child (Or
Your Brain-Damaged, Mentally Retarded, Mentally
Deficient, Cerebral Palsied, Spastic, Flaccid, Rigid,
Epileptic, Autistic, Athetoid, Hyperactive Child)**
Glenn Doman
Doubleday & Co., 245 Park Ave., NYC 10017 ($7.95)
Doman documents the story of the Institutes for the
Achievement of Human Potential and its controversial
methods of treatment for severely brain-damaged chil-
dren. Useful charts are included, outlining develop-
mental levels in language, touch and movement and

giving approximate ages at which these levels are achieved by the average as well as the moderately and severely brain-damaged child.

TWINS

If you're the new parent of twins, there's a group that you ought to know about. It's the National Organization of Mothers of Twins Clubs (5402 Amberwood Lane, Rockville, MD 20853). The purpose of the organization is to assist mothers and fathers of twins, and it has branches in many cities.

Mrs. Marion P. Meyer, the Executive Secretary of the national group, says that most mothers of twins feel that the double carriage is a waste of money because it is so expensive and can be used only for such a short time. Twin strollers are more useful and can be resold to mothers with younger children. The rest of the equipment twins need is the same as for all babies — except in twos: two beds, two car seats, two feeding tables.

One helpful piece of advice comes from the Mountain Plains Mothers of Twins Club, in their brochure, *Helpful Hints for New Mothers of Twins*. Rather than trying to tote two babies around to the kitchen, bathroom, and other rooms of the house, they suggest that you select one area, or room, of the house and convert it into a complete nursery, with all the furniture and equipment you need. It's easier to bring chores and feeding to the babies.

Most mothers of twins agree that caring for twin babies is much harder, but when the twins reach toddlerhood, they're easier to deal with because they become natural playmates for each other and can entertain one another. Things will get better!

BROCHURES OF INTEREST

And Then There Were Two
Bergen County Mothers of Twins Club, Child Study Association, 9 E. 89th St., NYC 10028 ($1.85)

Double Dilemma
Milwaukee Mothers of Twins Club, % Mrs. Eugene Schwartz, 5265 S. Tuckaway Dr., Greenfield, WI 53221 ($1.00)

Double Talk
No. Virginia Mothers of Twins Club, P.O. Box 3263, Alexandria, VA 22302

For Two, Please
Mainline Mothers of Twins Club, % Mrs. Bernard Luniffe, 441 Highland Ter., Holmes, PA 19043 ($1.25)

Helpful Hints for New Mothers of Twins
Mountain Plains Mothers of Twins Club, Corresponding Secretary, P.O. Box 351, Scotch Plains, NJ 07076 (50¢)

The Joy of Twins
Mothers of Twins Club of Buffalo, % Mrs. Fran Wisholek, 4282 Cherry Pl., Hamburg, NY 14075

A Message for New Twin Parents
Twins' Mothers' Club of Greater Plainfield, % Mrs. E. H. Kenstler, 14 Ninth St., RR 2, Warren, NJ 07060 (50¢)

No Two Alike
Ohio Federation Mothers of Twins Club, % Mrs. Eugene A. Pfeiffer, 946 17th St., N.E., Massillon, OH 44646

Tips for Twin Tots
Keystone Mothers of Twins Club, P.O. Box 234, Shiremanstown, PA 17011 ($1.00)

Twice upon a Time
Twins' Mothers' Club of Greater Hartford, P.O. Box 14244, Berry Square Station, Hartford, CT 06114 (50¢)

Twin Care . . . in a Nutshell
Massachusetts Mothers of Twins Association, Inc., 20 Appleton Rd., Natick, MA 01760 ($1.15)

Twins, Our World and Welcome to It
Greater Rochester Mothers of Twins Club, % Mrs. Kenneth McDonald, 18 Look Out View Rd., Fairport, NY 14450 (75¢)

Twins Are Two People
Mothers of Twins Club of Queens, % Mrs. Rose Savarese, 14–44 158th St., Beechurst, NY 11357 ($1.25)

Twins in Infancy
Twins' Mothers' Club of Westchester, % Mrs. M. R. Glick, 9 Downer Ave., Scarsdale, NY 10583 ($2.00)

Twin Tales
Waukesha Mothers of Twins Club, P.O. Box 1161, Waukesha, WI 53186 ($1.00)

Note: Not all manufacturers and publishers will accept single orders for a product or book. Always write them first, before sending money, to be certain that they will accept your order and make sure that you have the most recent price, including shipping and handling charges.

Back Packs

Carriers that attach a baby to its mother have been an age-old way of meeting a baby's need to be close to its mother while freeing the mother to do her work. The rhythm of walking and work has a soothing, relaxing effect on most babies. They seem serene and content while in a pack, as though the motion reminded them of those secure days before birth.

Back-packing will take some adjustment on your part, and it may seem to be quite a burden at first. It's wise to build up your carrying time over a period of days, rather than expecting to take a long hike as soon as you buy one. You will also need to practice loading and unloading Baby until you master the techniques gracefully and safely. The easiest way to begin is by backing into the baby-filled pack while it's supported by the back of a chair. It's important, too, that you practice getting the pack from ground level to your back and off again initially with someone's help. There will be many times when you won't have the convenience of your living room or a helping hand for loading and unloading your precious cargo.

You will probably find packing while hiking to be much more comfortable to your back and shoulders than it is when you shop or do household chores. Some mothers, though, have found their back packs to be very handy during the dinnertime rush, when babies are usually their fussiest.

Soft, fabric carriers seem to be the most suitable for the very young baby, since they usually have some type of head support. Young babies are more easily carried in the front. When your baby begins to hold herself erect (usually at about seven months of age), she's ready to graduate to an aluminum-frame carrier so that she can ride on your back while viewing the world over your shoulder.

Warning:
Improperly designed back packs have been found to constrict the circulation in a baby's legs seriously in as short a time as thirty minutes. Check to see that the leg holes of the pack are not higher than the level of the seat and that they do not leave deep pressure marks on Baby's legs. Immediately discontinue using a pack that causes Baby's legs to swell or turn blue. If your pack affects your baby's legs, don't forget to ask for a refund, to write the manufacturer, and to contact the Consumer Product Safety Commission (see the form at the end of the book). Here are the features to look for when purchasing your back pack:

● Shoulder straps should be firmly cushioned with foam. Try the pack on. The cushions should cover the muscle area of your shoulders on either side of your neck. This is the area that will bear most of your baby's weight.

● Check to see that the seat of the aluminum-frame carrier is deeply situated so that it places the baby midway down your back. This arrangement is safer, more stable, and helps to distribute Baby's weight off your shoulders.

● Check the aluminum-frame carrier to see that the metal tubing in front of Baby's face is covered and well padded.

● Check the baby's seating position in the aluminum-frame pack. She should be in a normal position, with her legs in front rather than squeezed under straps on the sides. How comfortable does the seating arrangement seem for Baby?

● Does the pack have a safety belt for securing an active toddler in the seat? Some babies enjoy climbing up into the seat and hovering precariously over their hosts' heads — a dangerous and difficult situation.

● The latches for adjusting the straps should hold securely and be simple to adjust.

● Finally, it's helpful if the fabric of the carrier is washable and wet-resistant.

A POORLY DESIGNED BACK PACK

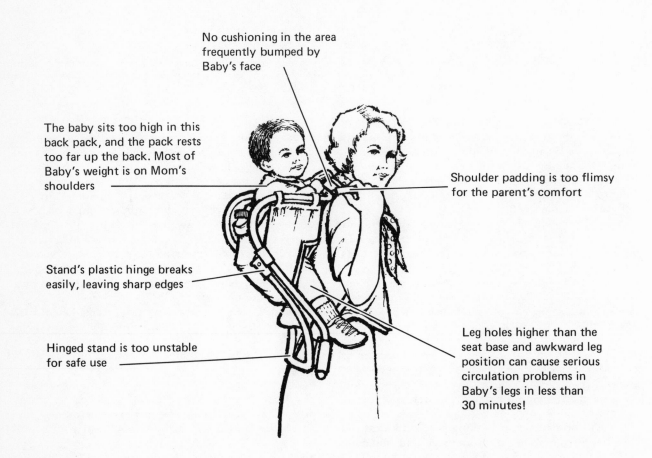

No cushioning in the area frequently bumped by Baby's face

The baby sits too high in this back pack, and the pack rests too far up the back. Most of Baby's weight is on Mom's shoulders

Shoulder padding is too flimsy for the parent's comfort

Stand's plastic hinge breaks easily, leaving sharp edges

Hinged stand is too unstable for safe use

Leg holes higher than the seat base and awkward leg position can cause serious circulation problems in Baby's legs in less than 30 minutes!

RECOMMENDED BACK PACKS

Andrea's Baby Pack

Some mothers find they prefer this carrier to the more expensive Snugli (see p. 12) because it is less bulky and cumbersome. The shoulder straps are padded and it has no zippers, snaps, or buckles, relying instead on sturdy, non-slip rings. The pack comes in a variety of bright, primary colors and has a gaily printed fabric interfacing. Order from:
Andrea's Baby Pack, 2441 Hilyard St., Eugene, OR 97405 (Approx. $28.00; write before ordering)

E-Z Baby Tote (*above*)

Although this carrier may seem a bit complicated to master at first, once it's on it comfortably supports not only the tiny baby but also the large, robust one, because the baby's weight is supported at the parent's waist rather than on the shoulders. Lightly padded shoulder straps and waist band. Washable, lightweight, and easy to store. Available in a variety of fabric colors and denim. Order from:
E-Z Enterprises, 901 N. Broadway, Wichita, KS 67214 ($13.50 + $1.50 postage and handling)

Hug'm Carrier (*above*)

This lightweight pack is designed to safely support the newborn baby's head. It also adjusts to accommodate babies up to about eight months of age. It is constructed of soft, brushed blue denim cotton. The carrier is machine washable and has a removable bib to protect itself and your clothing. Order from:
Coach House, P.O. Box 181, Victoria Station, Montreal, Quebec, Canada H3Z2V5 ($18.95 + $2.00 postage and handling; U.S. postage suffices)

Snugli

A superb, hand-crafted zipper pack with well-cushioned shoulder straps. Can be worn in front or back. Completely washable corduroy or seersucker with a changeable drool bib. Supports the head of the small infant; adjustable seat depth and darts make this carrier suitable also for larger toddlers. Choice of brilliant colors. Order, or ask for a brochure, from:
Snugli Cottage Industries, Inc., Route 1, Box 685, Evergreen, CO 80439 (Approx. $45.00)

Antelope Carrier

The Child Carrier is an accessory for the Antelope Packframe. It has a padded back and a solid seat suitable for serious hiking. The cost of the Child Carrier does not include pack frame and shipping costs. The frame, depending on the size of the wearer, costs between $30.00 and $50.00. The frame gives the advantage of padded shoulders and hip belt. It can also be used for other back-packing purposes. Send for a catalogue (25¢):
Antelope Camping Equipment, 21740 Granada Ave., Cupertino, CA 95014 ($16.80, seat only)

Happy Napsak

A front or back carrier of sturdy, cool net fabric. Can be used from two weeks through toddlerhood. Padded straps crisscross and tie in front or back. Adjustable, padded head-support panel. Order from:
Happy Family Products, 1252 S. La Cienega Blvd., Los Angeles, CA 90035 ($15.95 + $1.25 shipping)

PUBLICATIONS OF INTEREST

Baby Carrier
Packet No. 410
*La Leche League International, Inc., 9616 Minneapolis
Ave., Franklin Park, IL 60131 (50¢)*
Includes hints on use of baby carriers, actual patterns
for making carriers, slings, etc., and various flyers
describing commercially available baby carriers and
back packs.

Backpacking with Babies and Small Children
Goldie Silverman
*Signpost Publications, 16812 36th Ave. W., Lynnwood,
WA 98036 ($4.50)*
A guide to family camping for beginners. Of special
interest is a chapter on constructing your own back
packs, which includes instructions for making an
Indian-style back board.

Nursing Fashions
Packet No. 98
*La Leche League International, Inc., 9616 Minneapolis
Ave., Franklin Park, IL 60131 (50¢)*
Directions for do-it-yourself fabric baby carriers,
including a traditional Mexican carrier made from a
long shawl, and a Chinese *mai-tei* constructed from a
fabric square and four straps.

Note: Not all manufacturers and publishers will
accept single orders for a product or book. Always
write them first, before sending money, to be certain that they will accept your order and make
sure that you have the most recent price, including shipping and handling charges.

Bathing and Dental Care

Americans spend over $100 million a year on baby lotions, powders, and other baby toiletries. Mostly this is a needless waste of money, as these products are not necessary for the care of a baby's skin. A baby can have lovely, soft skin by being bathed only when he seems to need it. Baby skin has its own naturally protective oils, which overwashing strips away. Use just a little soap on hands and folds and avoid overwashing, particularly around the diaper area (unless your pediatrician suggests otherwise for diaper rash).

The only baby-care products that seem truly useful are a gentle soap, such as Johnson's Baby Soap, and a good, pasty, moisture-proof cream, such as Desitin Ointment (*not* Desenex), to form a protective layer wherever Baby shows irritation or redness. These products can be found at any drugstore. (*Do not* use soaking products or bath bubbles when bathing little ones; these products are harsh and can lead to genital inflammation.)

Be very careful in your use of baby powder. When inhaled in quantity it can cause a serious type of pneumonia in a baby. Never let your baby play with the baby-powder container and don't leave it within his reach. Cornstarch, which has a fine texture and is odorless, makes an excellent powder.

BATHING BABY

The most luxurious and natural way to bathe a baby is to take him in the tub with you. Be sure to purchase a bath mat or stick-on grids to prevent slipping. Draw the water beforehand and check it with your foot to be sure that it's comfortably warm. (Your hand will mislead you into thinking that the water's cooler than it really is.)

Turn the cold water spigot off last so that the faucet will not be hot should Baby touch it. *Never* turn the spigots on while Baby is in the tub. Hot tap water turned on by mistake can seriously scald a baby.

After filling the tub, undress yourself and then Baby. Put him in a baby seat or wrap him in a towel on the floor. Get in the tub yourself and then gently lift Baby over. Shampooing and other washing can be done with Baby lying face up on your legs with his head at your stomach. Keep his towel at hand so that you can pat him dry before lifting him out and getting out yourself.

It's important that you allow ample time during bathing and diapering to caress Baby gently, starting from his head down his body and out his arms and feet. A baby brush is excellent for gently stimulating back and front and helping him to become more aware of his body.

Remember: *Never* leave a baby or toddler unattended in water. (Even a few inches of water can be hazardous.) If you have to answer the phone, take Baby with you. When heartbreaking tragedies occur in the bathtub, almost always the mother reports, "I was only gone for a moment!"

BATHING AIDS

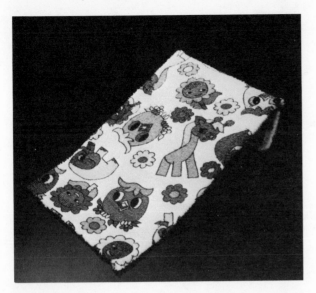

Bath-Eze

This washable terry sling slips snugly onto a sturdy vinyl-coated metal brace for bathing Baby in sink or adult tub. Parents like this invention because the angle of the sling frees their hands to soap and rinse Baby. Order from:
Reliance Products Corp., 108 Mason St., Woonsocket, RI 02895 ($6.95)

Bath Seat

The Deluxe Baby Anchor Bath Seat is for use in the adult bathtub by babies who can sit up (six months or older). The molded plastic seat has a foam cushion for Baby's bottom. The seat is held firmly to the tub by deep suction cups. Available in the infant section of department stores. Manufactured by:
Wallace, Davis Co., P.O. Box 4308, Hamden, CT 06514 (Approx. $6.00)

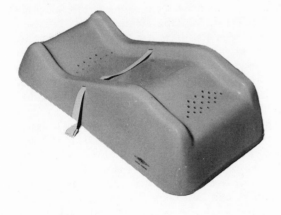

Shampooette

A rigid plastic support stand that can be used in the tub to bathe a small baby and later as a stand for shampooing a reclining child's hair. Baby's head rests on the higher section of the support. Shampooing a toddler's hair is a much-resisted event because he doesn't like to lie back in water. What an ingenious aid! Order from:
Roseal Co., 511 17th Ave., San Francisco, CA 94121 ($9.95 + $1.35 shipping)

Mother's Bath Apron

A terry apron with plastic backing to keep you dry while bathing Baby. Has a roomy pocket for toiletries and hairbrush. Order from:
The Comfy-Babe Co., P.O. Box 326, Downers Grove, IL 60515 ($8.00)

Nasal Aspirator
A helpful, gentle suction bulb for clearing out baby's nose when he's got a cold. Available at most pharmacies and drugstores. Manufactured by:
Davol, Inc., Box D, Providence, RI 02901 (Under $2.00)

Shampoo Shield
A flexible plastic ring in bright yellow for curing the toddler's shampoo blues! The ring slips right over the child's head to allow rinse water to go down his back instead of into his eyes. Write for a colorful free catalogue of baby products.
Mothercare-by-Mail, 196 Quaker Bridge Mall, U.S. Rt. 1 and Quaker Bridge Rd., Lawrenceville, NJ 08648 (Approx. $2.50)

German Baby Soap
Puhl's Kinder Seife Baby Soap is a gentle, fragrant bar for bathing Baby. It comes gift-boxed. Trüc also carries a delightful set of unpainted animal-shaped soaps for tots made with olive oil and lanolin. Write for a catalogue.
The Soap Box at Trüc, P.O. Box 167, Woodstock Hill, CT 06281 (Baby Soap approx. $1.65 a box)

DENTAL CARE

Shelden Bernick, D.D.S., in an article published in *Clinical Pediatrics* (September 1970) suggests the following procedures in caring for Baby's teeth:
• Prior to eighteen months of age, a baby's teeth should be cleaned daily with a piece of gauze or cotton moistened with hydrogen peroxide and flavored with a few drops of mouthwash. Baby's gums are too tender to be brushed at this age. (Keep the peroxide out of your tot's reach — it's not for drinking!)
• Starting at eighteen months, parents should brush Baby's teeth with a small, soft, nylon-bristle toothbrush and regular toothpaste.
• After brushing, turn the toothbrush over to your tot to let him practice by imitating you as you brush your teeth. Teeth should be brushed in the same direction that they grow — down for upper teeth and up for lower teeth. Scrub back and forth on biting surfaces (such as the tops of molars). Then rinse the mouth out with water.

Parents have found that using an electric toothbrush is easier, although children under five can't handle one themselves. The best electric brushes are cordless and shock-proof and provide an up-and-down motion.

The American Academy of Pediatrics, in a joint report with the American Society of Dentistry for Children, points out that cavities seldom occur when the daily diet contains no refined sugar and minimal carbohydrates. One study found that children who had better diets, with more fresh fruits and vegetables, had fewer cavities than those who ate a lot of candies and sweets, particularly between meals. It suggests that, if your child insists on eating candy, you let him have it at the end of the meal, rather than in between meals, when it is more likely to cause decay.

PUBLICATIONS AND PRODUCTS OF INTEREST

"Dental Caries and the Consideration of the Role of Diet in Prevention"

American Academy of Pediatrics, Box P, P.O. Box 1034, Evanston, IL 60204 (50¢)
A rather technical reprint from *Pediatrics* magazine that explains what causes cavities and reviews research in the prevention of tooth decay. You might also write for the Academy's publications list.

"A Preventive Care Guide for Multihandicapped Children: Dental Care Begins at Home"

Albert Green, D.D.S.
National Easter Seal Society for Crippled Children and Adults, 2023 W. Ogden Ave., Chicago, IL 60612 (Single copies free)
A brief, clearly written article on tooth care and decay prevention reprinted from *Rehabilitation Literature* that stresses the role of diet. A brochure listing other Easter Seal publications is available upon request.

Your Child's Teeth

Stephen J. Moss, D.D.S.
Houghton Mifflin Co., 2 Park St., Boston, MA 02107 ($3.95, paperback)
A primer for parents, this information-packed book will tell you how to care for your baby's and tot's teeth, how to treat a toothache until you can get to the dentist, how to avoid nursing-bottle mouth, the meaning of tooth stains, and much more. Excellent!

Note: Not all manufacturers and publishers will accept single orders for a product or book. Always write them first, before sending money, to be certain that they will accept your order and make sure that you have the most recent price, including shipping and handling charges.

THE DANGERS OF AN OLDER CRIB

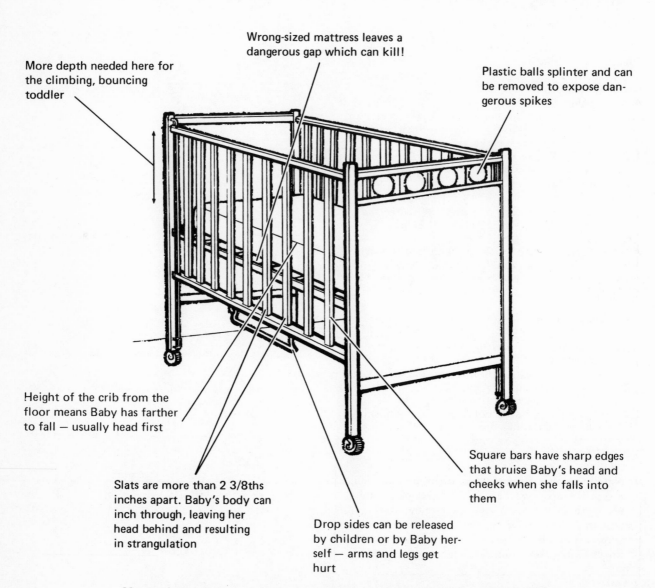

More depth needed here for the climbing, bouncing toddler

Wrong-sized mattress leaves a dangerous gap which can kill!

Plastic balls splinter and can be removed to expose dangerous spikes

Height of the crib from the floor means Baby has farther to fall — usually head first

Slats are more than 2 3/8ths inches apart. Baby's body can inch through, leaving her head behind and resulting in strangulation

Drop sides can be released by children or by Baby herself — arms and legs get hurt

Square bars have sharp edges that bruise Baby's head and cheeks when she falls into them

Most serious injuries and deaths from cribs have occurred in older, broken cribs

Beds and Accessories

CRIBS

The crib as we know it is a new and novel device. Historically, members of the human race gathered warmly together to sleep. Baby and mother slept together, with the baby nursing whenever she wanted to throughout the night. It is only in very recent history — the past hundred years, perhaps — that it has become the mode to put Baby in a room to herself, in a wooden cage (the crib) and to give her a bottle rather than her mother's warmth. This separation of baby and mother seems quite unnatural compared to the skin-to-skin contact that has been the birthright of all animals and most human babies to date — and still is, in less "civilized" countries.

The crib is a highly dangerous contraption. In the early 1970s the U.S. Consumer Product Safety Commission estimated that as many as 200 babies a year were being killed in crib-related accidents and that another 50,000 were injured seriously enough to need emergency-room care. In 1974 the Commission instituted regulations for all full-sized cribs, and since then crib-related injuries have been reduced by as much as 44 per cent.

Although many of the design errors in cribs have now been eliminated, I still feel uneasiness about the way we westerners cage babies in separate rooms and then blame them for their lusty objections. Once we understand that the baby needs continual, close, intimate physical contact, we can devise more responsive patterns for dealing with our babies: sleeping with them, nursing them, carrying them on our bodies. A good deal of loving, energy, and sensuousness should be exchanged between a baby and her caregivers. When we

abort that connection, we, the parents, lose a wonderful experience.

What can a concerned parent do? Probably the most practical approach for most families is to select a new crib and then to pad and cushion it well. Another possibility is to put your new baby in a well-padded baby carriage next to your bed, or in a padded drawer placed safely on a solid table. One mother of twins used an extra-large woven laundry basket, which was marvelously portable, too. Some parents have used a mattress or pad placed directly on the floor. The major disadvantage of floor sleeping for a baby or tot is that you don't have the security of knowing that your little one is safely restrained while you sleep.

Here are some features to look for when purchasing a new crib:

- Choose rounded slats over squared ones, if possible.
- Choose a single-drop-sided crib rather than a double-drop-side design and plan to leave the sides permanently *up*. (Single-drop-sided cribs are more stable, but difficult to find these days.)
- Look for a metal stabilization bar that runs from one headboard to the other underneath the springs. This ensures a sturdier crib.
- For added safety, keep the mattress support at its lowest position.
- Check for firmly attached, flexible teething rails that will not split, pull off, or break. The wood surface under the railings should be finished and splinter-free. Rigid plastic railings sometimes break into long slivers that can cut fingers and injure eyes. (Anyway, babies are smart; they'll chew on the end of the bed, or wherever they can find wood.)
- Test the operation of the drop sides by raising and

FEDERAL REQUIREMENTS FOR FULL-SIZE BABY CRIBS

• *The interior dimensions of the crib shall be 28 inches wide as measured from the innermost surfaces of the crib and 52 3/8 inches long (give or take 5/8 inch).* The prime reason for this ruling is to ensure a firm fit between the crib and the mattress by standardizing crib sizes. Very young babies can trap their heads in the gap between the end of the mattress and the end of the crib, causing death from strangulation.

• *There should be at least 9 inches between the mattress support in its highest position and the top of the drop side in its lowest position.* (*Drop side* means the side of the crib on which railings go up and down.) Babies may tumble out of cribs if the sides are too low to protect them from falls.

• *There should be at least 26 inches between the mattress support in its lowest position and the top of the rails or end panels in their highest position.* This prevents standing and jumping babies from falling out or climbing out of the crib.

• *There should be no more than 2 3/8 inches between crib rods, or between rods and corner posts.* (The width of three adult fingers is roughly equivalent to this measurement.) Babies' small, flexible bodies can slip through the railings on some cribs, leaving their necks wedged between the bars and causing death by strangulation.

• *Hardware on the crib should not cause bruising, cutting, pinching, or other injuries to users.* Screws, clamps, and other metal devices on the crib sometimes cause injury when babies fall against them.

• *Locking or latching devices that hold drop-side railings should require at least 10 pounds of force to make them release.* Brothers, sisters, pets, and even babies themselves can accidentally make the sides of cribs fall, causing dangerous falls from the crib.

• *Wood surfaces should be smooth and free of splinters.*

• *Cribs should not have a bar or ledge that a baby can use for climbing out.* Any ledges on the crib must be placed more than 20 inches above the mattress support in its lowest position and the side rail in its highest position. Babies may use crib decorations and ridges to climb out of the crib and then tumble headfirst onto the floor.

• *Cribs shipped unassembled from the factory should have clear, detailed instructions, along with warnings about keeping the bolts safely fastened once the crib is assembled. A warning should be included that the crib should not be used by children over 35 inches tall.* Parents may assemble cribs incorrectly, causing hardware to bend and break. Children are apt to get hurt when they outgrow their cribs and attempt to climb in and out of them.

lowering them repeatedly. Sides should go up and down easily, without jamming.

• Avoid cribs with decorative decals; these often peel when they are wiped clean or exposed to excess moisture from a humidifier.

• Does the crib seem sturdy when it's given a good shaking?

• Is everything firmly attached, including each slat and all hardware?

• Are there any sharp or rough edges that could injure a falling baby?

RECOMMENDED CRIBS

Crib Pattern

Complete instructions on a full-sized drawing for constructing your own crib of birch or maple. Includes directions for making all operating hardware. (Suggestion: Make the crib with round dowels, rather than square ones, and leave the sides firmly up rather than drop-sided. You might wish to build the crib closer to the floor for safety's sake.) Order Pattern No. 500 from: *Furniture Designs, 1425 Sherman Ave., Evanston, IL 60201 ($7.00)*

Convertible Crib

Available in pine grain Formica or pure white laminated Formica, this innovative crib has an acrylic end panel to let Baby see out. Later, the bed can be converted to a youth bed, complete with a guard rail on both sides. Order from the catalogue of:
Children's Design Center, 29 Excelsior Springs Ave., Saratoga Springs, NY 12866 ($210.00 Freight Collect)

Protex-A-Matt

A shield that goes between the mattress and the crib springs to prevent rust spots or tearing of the mattress cover. Tailored to fit any crib, it can be folded away when the crib's not in use. For "where to find it" information or to order, write:
Stephen Shanan Co., 10107 Westview 211, Houston, TX 77043 ($2.95 + postage and handling)

Chrome Crib

A shiny chrome crib designed for institutions like hospitals. It meets the U.S. Consumer Product Safety Commission's standards. For added durability, this crib has only one drop side. The opposite side can be removed, allowing both ends of the crib to fold for easy storage. The rounded bars are a nice feature, too. A smaller, portable model, which is shorter and narrower with telescoping legs, is available. Write for information:
Major-Lab Manufacturing, 4420 North Sewell, OK 73118 (Standard size, #1392, or Portable, #1389, $253.45 plus shipping)

CRIB BUMPERS

Crib bumpers are an important safety and comfort investment for Baby. They protect her from becoming wedged in the bars and give some cushioning for the special corner that little babies like to push their heads into. Vinyl-covered foam bumpers "aren't worth a nickel," as my grandmother would say. The seams tear and the ties pull off. Bumpers should be taken out of the crib as soon as Baby begins to use them as a prop for pulling up, since they will collapse and send her head into the railings. The best bumpers for the money are firmly padded fabric models. Check to see that the bumper has at least six ties for fastening it to the crib. Once you have tied the bumper onto the railings, clip off excess streamers so that the baby won't get entangled in them.

Fabric Bumpers and Accessories
Bring out the ginghams, calicoes, and bright colors! The soft, fabric crib bumpers are nice to the touch, and washable, too. This company and several others now make matching fabric bumpers, quilts, dust ruffles, and other crib finery. (For safety and comfort, don't use a pillow for Baby.)
Noel Joanna, Inc., 23251 Vista Grande, Laguna Hills, CA 92653

CRADLES

Perhaps you'd like to consider buying or making a cradle. The cradle has such a romantic aura surrounding it. When I became pregnant, I fell in love with a giant cradle, and we bought it on the spot. Imagine the two of us trying to fit it through our tiny apartment doors. I couldn't wait to rock the baby in it! Unfortunately, the cradle's motion rolled our little one from one side to the other. When she grew bigger, her weight would cause the cradle to shift unpredictably, and she would end up jammed against the side. We finally propped a large book under one rocker to stabilize it when we didn't want it to move. I bruised my shins many a night on its long rockers while groping around in the dark. Still, I remember our cradle as a symbol of that romantic feeling of being a new mother.

Here are some pros and cons of cradle buying. First, like a baby carriage, a cradle has a limited length of use in view of its high cost. For safety's sake, you should stop using one when the baby begins attempting to pull up on the corners (at six to seven months of age), because the sides are dangerously low. Cradles can't be folded, or packed away easily, which might be an important factor if you live in an apartment or plan to be moving frequently. On the other hand, cradles have excellent resale value. And what could be more cherished than a handmade cradle passed down from generation to generation?

Here are some considerations to keep in mind when selecting a cradle:
● Avoid cradles suspended by hooks. These protruding metal pieces are hazardous when Baby is being put in the cradle, particularly in the dark.
● Solid sides are safer than slatted sides and preferred by very young babies.
● The best buy is a cradle suspended from a frame, particularly one that can be locked into a nonrocking position.

CRADLES AND CRADLE PATTERNS

Berea Cradle

A reproduction of a cradle first made by Wallace Nutting in the early twentieth century, featuring exquisitely turned spindles and legs. It's crafted by the students of Berea College in cherry, mahogany, or walnut. Order four to six months in advance (and for safety's sake, specify that the spindles be no more than 2⅜" apart). For ordering information, write:
Manager, Log House Sales Room, Berea College Student Craft Industries, P.O. Box 2347, Berea, KY 40404 (Approx. $250.00)

Double-Action Cradle Pattern

A suspended cradle that is pivoted to swing and mounted on rockers as well. It accommodates a standard baby-carriage pad. The pattern shows parts in actual size. Once you have traced the pattern onto wood and sawed it out, assembling is easy. Order Pattern No. 2104 from:
Craft Patterns, 2200 Dean St., St. Charles, IL 60174 ($2.00)

Locking Cradle Pattern

A two-sheet plan shows how to make this cradle with either spindles or panel sides. It features a locking "key" such that the cradle need not swing if you so desire. Size: 20" × 39" × 30" high. Order Pattern No. 166 from:
Furniture Designs, 1425 Sherman Ave., Evanston, IL 60201 ($6.00)

Early American Cradle Pattern

Made from pine lumber, this old-fashioned cradle can be built with simple hand tools from a full-sized pattern. It's large and deep, with broad, nontipping rockers curved just enough to lull Baby gently to sleep. Once outgrown, it can be used as a container for firewood, magazines, or toys. Order Pattern No. 1347 from:
Craft Patterns, 2200 Dean St., St. Charles, IL 60174 ($2.00)

Cradle-to-Desk Combination

A cradle that becomes a toy-storage unit! Its frame becomes a youngster's desk. The cradle is made of cotton on a wooden frame. The desk top, which can be adjusted to three heights, has a blackboard finish on one side. (Pandas, quilts, and other play pretties are also available in the Design Center catalogue.)
Children's Design Center, 29 Excelsior Springs Ave., Saratoga Springs, NY 12866 ($165.00 + $10.00 shipping)

Hand-loomed Crib and Carriage Robe

Woven by students earning their way through Berea College, this baby-soft blanket has a Bronson pattern and fringe on all sides. Size: 36" × 45". Comes in blue, white, or pink. A lovely gift for Baby! Write for catalogues (furniture, $1.00; handcrafts, 25¢) and order from:
Berea College Student Craft Industries, Customer Service, P.O. Box 2347, Berea, KY 40404 ($17.95)

ACCESSORIES

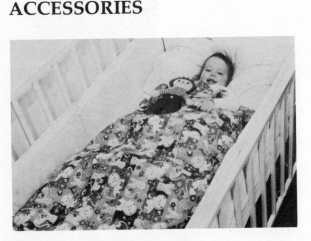

Baby-Sized Down Comforter Kit

From your own materials, you can make a lightweight but very warm coverlet that can be easily removed for washing. Included in the kit are uniquely designed plastic packets containing prime northern goose down, a fabric casing, thread, and instructions. An easy one-night project! Size: 28" × 40". Write for a catalogue.
Frostline Kits, Frostline Circle, Denver, CO 80241 ($28.95)

Papoose Snap Blanket

Invented by a mother, the Papoose blanket snaps to cover Baby's feet and to enclose her so snugly that she can kick without loosing it. Ideal for carrying baby infant seats, and carriages. It snaps to larger sizes as Baby grows. A variety of patterns and prices available.
Sweet Petite, Rte. 4, Harrisville Rd., Mt. Airy, MD 21771 ($9.00–$13.00)

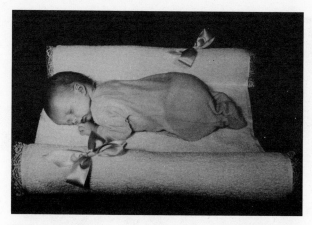

Baby Safe-Nap

Two soft, foam-filled bolsters slide into each side of a fabric blanket to make a portable sleeping area for a very young baby. The bolsters can be removed and used later as a bumper for a toddler's crib. Look in the babies' department of retail stores. Manufactured by: *Plakie Toys, Inc., P.O. Box 3386, Youngstown, OH 44512 ($10.00–$13.00, depending on fabric)*

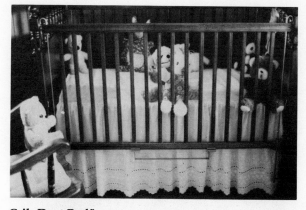

Crib Dust Ruffle

These washable cotton-polyester ruffles fit standard-sized cribs and are a good way to hide under-the-crib storage. Available in green, yellow, pink, blue, or red gingham, solid white, pink, or blue, and a more expensive white eyelet. Order from: *Ruffles Unlimited, Box 252, Horseheads, NY 14845 (Ginghams and solids, $18.00 + $1.95 postage; eyelet, $30.00 + $1.95 postage)*

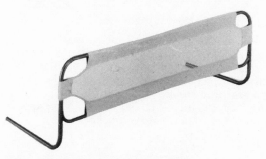

Safety Mesh Bed Railing (47–154)

A beige nylon net panel makes this bed railing a good adaptor for regular-sized beds. (Bed railings with widely spaced crossbars are dangerous, since tots can crawl through them, entrapping their heads.) The finish of the metal is nontoxic enamel. Side bars fit between the mattress and springs. Folds flat for travel and storage. Available in juvenile departments of stores, or order from: *Cosco Home Products, 2525 State St., Columbus, OH 47201 ($14.00)*

Bullrush Baby Basket

This easy-to-carry French traditional basket measures approximately 29" long by 19" wide and 18" tall. It is woven from natural palm and cane reed. The instructions for making the liner are included or you may order an optional two-piece quilted gingham liner and coverlet. Order from: *New Orleans Baby Co., Dept. GT-B, P.O. Box 4190, New Orleans, LA 70118 (Basket, $35.00; gingham liner and coverlet, $13.00)*

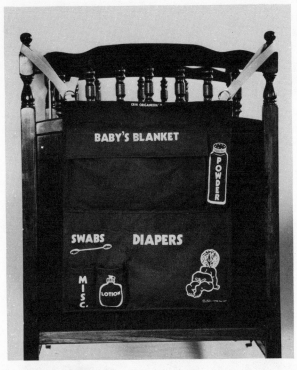

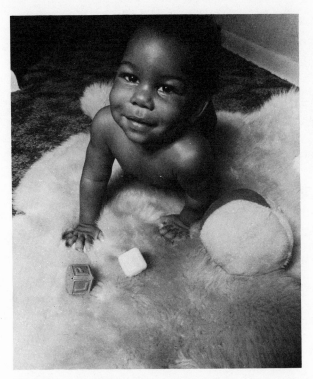

Crib Organizer

A pocket for everything! This washable fabric hold-all has a place for all of Baby's odds and ends. It can be fastened to the wall, the back of the door, or the crib itself. Colors: natural, yellow, or navy, with a variety of print colors. Order from:
C.P. & M. Corp., P.O. Box 1782, Akron, OH 44309 ($13.50)

Baby Care Lambskin

A plush, washable lambskin is a super way to soothe a small baby. The skin has been clinically sterilized and chosen for its texture. It can be used in the crib, on the floor, or as a quick signal for naptime while traveling. Write for a brochure and up-to-date price:
Health Care Products, Inc., P.O. Box 26221, Denver, CO 80226 (Approx. $35.00 plus postage and handling)

FOR FURTHER READING

"Common Causes of Baby's Night Crying and Sleeplessness"

Dr. Gustave Weinfold
Order from: Service Editor, Baby Talk *Magazine, 66 E. 34th St., NYC 10016 (30¢ + 75¢ service charge)*
A reprint of an article appearing in *Baby Talk* that discusses and suggests solutions to almost every question about Baby's sleep that might puzzle a new parent.

Crib Safety: Keep Them on the Safe Side

U.S. Consumer Product Safety Commission Publication No. 6305-74, Washington, DC 20207 (Free)
A leaflet describing the regulations of the U.S. Consumer Product Safety Commission regarding cribs. Tells what to look for in buying a new crib, or in fixing up an older crib, and gives sound safety suggestions.

Note: Not all manufacturers and publishers will accept single orders for a product or book. Always write them first, before sending money, to be certain that they will accept your order and make sure that you have the most recent price, including shipping and handling charges.

Books and Music for Babies and Toddlers

Little ones enjoy books, first as a touching experience, and later for listening and remembering familiar things. Toddlers love to be read to, perhaps because it gives the security of being close to a loved parent. Books can help to stimulate language development and provide experiences for the baby, just as toys do.

Babies should never be allowed to mouth or chew fabric or paper books, magazines, or newspapers. The Australian Consumer's Association, running tests for toxic levels of lead in the coloring matter of fabric baby books, did find lead in them, ranging from traces to dangerously high amounts. Full-color advertisements in magazines also have poisonous lead in them.

The ideal book for a baby has brilliantly colored photographs of familiar things, animals, babies, and children on heavy cardboard pages. Avoid any plastic spiral bindings with teeth that are not glued to the spine. Such bindings are brittle and can easily break into small pieces that may be swallowed. Fabric and plastic-sheeted books are also unsuitable, because it's difficult for babies to turn the pages and the edges frequently cut small fingers.

Abstract or unclear sketches of animals and people might appeal to adults buying the book but are difficult for little ones to decipher. It's best to buy books with large, clear, realistic pictures and only one central idea on each page.

Outdated wallpaper books are usually free for the asking from paint stores. They make excellent first books for crawling babies. The colors are bright, and many samples have interesting geometric patterns and unusual textures. These books are large and bulky, but babies enjoy sitting on them and examining the pages. No tasting or chewing allowed!

HOW TO MAKE YOUR OWN BOOK

It's easy to make a book for Baby containing pictures of things that he loves. To make your book, cut out pictures from magazines, catalogues, gift wrapping, and product boxes. People and pet photos will appeal to Baby, too. Color pictures are better than black and white.

Use sturdy, colored poster board for the book's pages. Place one picture on each page and then cover the pages with transparent Con-Tact paper. Round the corners with scissors. Punch two holes in the book and lace the pages together with scraps of bright yarn.

Homemade fabric books are also a pleasure to lap-sitting toddlers. Each page can have a task for a little one to do, such as a large button and flap with a button-hole; a buckle; or laces to thread through holes. Or, you may choose to make a book of animals from a variety of textures and fabrics. At least one major pattern company offers a pattern for a fabric book with marvelous creatures in it.

BOOKS FOR OLDER BABIES AND TODDLERS

Some of the characteristics of a good book for an older baby or toddler are: bright, uncomplicated full-page illustrations, a text of only a few sentences at most on each page, and words that play on sounds and flow smoothly. Here follows a list of super books for lap reading. The asterisked titles are so special that I recommend them for purchase for your favorite tot's beginning book collection.

*Animals on the Farm

Feodor Rojanovsky
Alfred A. Knopf, 201 E. 50th St., NYC 10022 ($5.99)
For the baby learning the names of animals, this book is realistically illustrated with a single word label in large letters on each page.

Ape in a Cape

Fritz Eichenberg
Harcourt, Brace, Jovanovich, 751 Third Ave., NYC 10017 ($4.95)
An alphabet book of funny animals that emphasizes phonetic sounds: for example, "goat in a boat" and "fox in a box."

Father Fox's Pennyrhymes

Clyde Watson
Thomas Y. Crowell Co., 666 Fifth Ave., NYC 10019 ($6.95)
Marvelous, silly animal rhymes that will start you both giggling.

*Goodnight Moon

Margaret Wise Brown
Harper & Row, 10 E. 53rd St., NYC 10022 ($4.95, $1.50, paperback)
A dear little bunny, a toddler, no doubt, says goodnight to all the things in his room. Look for other great books for the very young by Brown, especially *A Child's Goodnight Book*, which tells about animals going to sleep.

On Mother's Lap

Ann Herbert Scott
McGraw-Hill Book Co., 1221 Ave. of the Americas, NYC 10020 ($6.95)
A gentle story of a little Eskimo child and his relationship to his mother and the new baby in his house.

*Pat the Bunny

Dorothy Kunhardt
Western Publishing Co., 850 Third Ave., NYC 10022 ($3.95)
A perennial favorite — even when we were kids! The book has things to touch, such as daddy's whiskers, a bunny to pat, and a perfumed flower to smell. The perfect giftbook for a little one.

Play with Me

Marie Hall Ets
Viking Press, 625 Madison Ave., NYC 10022 ($4.95)
A two-year-old tries to make friends with the creatures in a meadow.

*Sleep, Baby, Sleep

Trudi Oberhänsli
Atheneum Publishers, 122 E. 42nd St., NYC 10017 ($4.95)
The old lullabye illustrated with magnificent, richly colored full-page paintings. Very simple wording, with the music at the end. A perfect Christmas gift for a tot.

The Snowy Day

Ezra Jack Keats
Viking Press, 625 Madison Ave., NYC 10022 ($5.95)
A book that is artistically pleasing in its collages of patterns and colors. About a small boy and the snow. Look for the many other titles by Keats in the library.

*The Tall Book of Mother Goose

Feodor Rojanovsky
Western Publishing Co., 850 Third Ave., NYC 10022 ($5.49)
The best! You may remember this exquisite book from your own childhood. The beautiful illustrations of Mother Goose rhymes make it a classic.

Whose Mouse Are You?

Robert Kraus; Illustrated by Jose Aruego
Macmillan Publishing Co., 866 Third Ave., NYC 10022 ($7.95)
A simple rhyming story in which a mouse answers questions about his missing family. Bright, fun-filled drawings.

FINGER PLAY BOOKS

Finger plays are fun for tots and parents to do together. They also help to develop a young child's finger and hand coordination.

Finger Play Fun
Violette Steiner and Roberta Pond
Charles E. Merrill Publishing Co., 1300 Alum Creek Dr., Columbus, OH 43216 ($6.95)

Fingerplays
Marianne Yamaguchi
Holt, Rinehart & Winston, 383 Madison Ave., NYC 10017 (95¢, paperback)

Finger Plays and Action Rhymes
Frances E. Jacobs
Lothrop, Lee & Shepard Co., 105 Madison Ave., NYC 10016 ($4.95)

Finger Plays for Nursery and Kindergarten
Emilie Poulsson
Dover Publications, 180 Varick St., NYC 10014 ($1.50, paperback)

Let's Do Fingerplays
Marion Grayson
Robert B. Luce, 2000 N St., N.W., Washington, DC 20036 ($5.50)

Rhymes for Fingers and Flannelboards
Louise B. Scott
McGraw-Hill Book Co., 1221 Ave. of the Americas, NYC 10020 ($7.95)

BOARD BOOKS FOR BABIES

The Children's Book and Music Center has an excellent collection of board books for babies. Included in the collection are the Dick Bruna books, such as *B Is for Bear* ($4.95), Gyo Fujikawa's *My Favorite Thing* ($2.50), and a collection of six photo board books with pictures of household things, children, and toys (6 for $5.88). Write for a catalogue listing up-to-date prices:

Children's Book and Music Center, 5373 W. Pico Blvd., Los Angeles, CA 90019 (Catalogue, $1.00)

GUIDEBOOKS FOR CHILDREN'S READING MATERIALS

A Parent's Guide to Children's Reading
Nancy Larrick
Bantam Books, 666 Fifth Ave., NYC 10019 ($1.95, paperback)
Hundreds of books are reviewed in this superb handbook, including nursery rhymes, picture books, ABC and counting books, magazines, songbooks, and records. There are also discussions of television and children and of children's early language development.

Whole Child/Whole Parent
Polly Berrien Berends
Harper's Magazine Press, 10 East 53rd St., NYC 10022 ($6.95)
Ms. Berends reviewed between 3000 and 5000 books to present her choice of nearly 500 books for children under four. The books have brief descriptions and are categorized by levels to help parents in choosing books appropriate to their child's level. Superior books that make good purchases are also noted. The book also presents a philosophical approach to child-rearing and gives hints for purchasing products.

MUSIC FOR BABIES AND TODDLERS

SONG BOOKS

For a complete listing of song books for children see *Subject Guide to Books in Print,* under the heading "Children's Songs." Asterisked books are recommended as gifts.

*The Baby's Song Book

Elizabeth Poston, Ed.
Thomas Y. Crowell Co., 666 Fifth Ave., NYC 10019
($7.95)
Eighty traditional nursery songs with piano arrangements and full-color illustrations. Only mediocre piano-playing skills needed.

The Fireside Book of Children's Songs

Marie Winn, Ed.
Simon & Schuster, 630 Fifth Ave., NYC 10020 ($9.95)
Songs about animals, nursery rhymes, and silly songs like "I Know an Old Lady Who Swallowed a Fly."

*The Golden Song Book

Katherine T. Wessells, Ed.
Western Publishing Co., 850 Third Ave., NYC 10022
($3.95)
A real bargain! All the very favorite songs, with beautiful Golden Book illustrations throughout. Remember "Twinkle, Twinkle Little Star" and "Old Macdonald Had a Farm"?

Lullabies and Night Songs

William Engvick, Ed.
Harper & Row, 10 E. 53rd St., NYC 10022 ($15.00)
Forty-eight lullabies and songs with new melodies. The illustrations are by Maurice Sendak. Expensive — look for it in your library.

1000 Jumbo: The Children's Song Book

Charles Hansen, Distributor, 1860 Broadway, NYC 10023
($19.95)
A giant telephone-book-sized volume filled with every song imaginable. It's paperback, and the songs are all spelled out with single notes. There's a section on how to play a recorder, directions for piano playing, and even guitar instructions. This book could be a hobby all by itself!

RECORDS FOR TODDLERS

Lullabye from the Womb

Dr. Hajime Murooka, a Japanese physician, has recorded the noises within the womb of an expectant mother. Supposedly the gurgling and boomping is soothing to a newborn baby, who feels quite at home with the din. Also included are traditional symphonic pieces for soothing older babies and harried parents. For more information, write:
Capitol Records, Inc., The Capitol Tower, P.O. Box 2391, Hollywood, CA 90028 (Record, $6.98; cassette, $7.98)

The Children's Book and Music Center, Inc., is an excellent source by mail for records for the very young. Here are some record albums that they suggest for the very young child:

Israeli Folk Dances

Vigorous, rhythmic dance songs and music that stimulate even a baby to dance, clap, and laugh ($7.98).

Music for the 1's and 2's

Songs for the very young sung by Tom Glazer. Includes "Where are Your Eyes?," "Big and Little," and "Clap Hands" (Record, $6.98; cassette, $7.95).

A Child's First Record

Frank Luther's songs about games, pets, and toys with music and sound effects for the very young ($4.98).

Nursery and Mother Goose Songs

Simple, childlike arrangements of "Little Jack Horner," "Three Little Kittens," "Rock a 'Bye Baby" and other favorites for tots ($6.96).

Songs to Grow on for Mother and Child

Songs and games for the whole family composed and sung by Woody Guthrie ($6.98).

Activity Songs

Original songs by Marica Berman, such as "I'm Not Small," "Choo Choo," and others ($5.98).

Folk Song Carnival

Songs recorded by Hap Palmer including "Hush Little Baby," "Going to the Zoo," and other simple tunes ($7.95, record or cassette).

Write for the catalogue of books and records ($1.00) at this address:

Children's Book and Music Center, Inc., 5373 W. Pico Blvd., Los Angeles, CA 90019

Barnyard Animals

A toddler's delight of actual animal sounds including cows, chicks, horses, and ducks. Other albums are available with bird calls, the sounds of the meadows, swamps, and the sea. Write for a free leaflet.
Droll Yankees, Inc., Mill Road, Foster, RI 02825
(Barnyard Animals, $2.00)

Note: Not all manufacturers and publishers will accept single orders for a product or book. Always write them first, before sending money, to be certain that they will accept your order and make sure that you have the most recent price, including shipping and handling charges.

Breastfeeding Helps

If you want to succeed in breastfeeding your baby, it's important to decide *before* your baby comes. Try to read all you can about breastfeeding. Make friends with mothers who have had long nursing relationships with their own babies. And, if at all possible go to several La Leche (pronounced *Lay chay*) League meetings while you're pregnant and later with your new baby. Well-informed League leaders will answer your questions and help you to overcome any doubts you may have about breastfeeding. There's a League number to call in most cities that will refer you to an experienced mother, or call the national number in Illinois: (312) 455–7730.

Unfortunately, however, there are subtle pressures *against* breastfeeding that may dissuade a mother even if she secretly would like to breastfeed. Glossy men's magazines have succeeded in convincing us that breasts are solely sexual — somehow naughty and secret. A mother nursing her baby — an event viewed with awe in other countries — is seen as embarrassing and a bit indecent in the U.S., whereas a mother giving her baby a bottle is given full public acceptance. Relatives are the first to ask "When do you plan to wean your baby?" as though this natural feeding were harmful to the baby or might make her too dependent.

Many members of the medical profession have been "sold" on formulas by the giant baby-food industry. Mothers of very young breastfed babies are encouraged to give their infants supplemental formulas and cereal, even though babies thrive on breastmilk alone for at least six months. This procedure directly affects the amount of milk produced by a mother, since breastmilk production is ruled almost totally by how much and how often the baby nurses, not by breast size or nervousness of the mother as is commonly believed. A baby filled with supplemental formula and cereal is going to want to nurse less. She may even begin to prefer the ease of sucking on a rubber nipple to the hard work of coaxing milk out of Mom's breast. The less the baby nurses, the less milk Mom makes and the more bottle she gets — thus begins the cycle of early weaning.

Don't judge nursing by your first two weeks of it! Your body is having to make many adjustments. Your glands are churning up for the work ahead, and your nipples may be a bit sore as they toughen up for feeding. (Sore nipples can be caused by a mild monilia infection. Check with your doctor. You can get temporary relief by continuous applications of a washcloth filled with crushed ice or by using cotton squares that have been moistened and then frozen.) The best part of nursing comes later, when you and Baby work together in perfect harmony. You'll never forget the tender moments sitting with Baby nestled close to you. It's a feeling of love and joy that's rarely duplicated in any other human experience!

NURSING AIDS

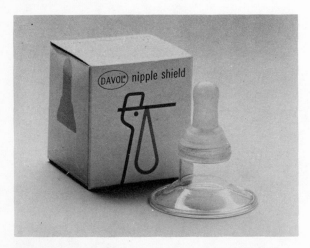

Davol Breast Shields

The Davol Company makes two types of breast shields. One, made of pure latex and shaped to fit directly over a portion of the breast and nipple, is designed to protect the nipple from chafing when sore during the first weeks of nursing. (Note: Exposing your breasts to air is probably the best treatment for this problem.) The second breast shield consists of a nipple attached to a plastic cup. It may provide temporary relief when you're have nipple problems. It allows Baby to nurse through the shield rather than directly on the breast. Please remember that these shields should be used sparingly, as a temporary measure only. The best advice is probably to "bite the bullet" and let your baby's sucking toughen your nipples for you. It's important that Baby nurse directly on your breast to stimulate milk production. Available at most pharmacies. For "where to find it" information, write:
Davol, Inc., P.O. Box D, Providence, RI 02901

The "Netsy" Swedish Milk Cup and Breast Shield

A transparent, dome-shaped plastic cover for the nipple that serves to collect leaking milk. Leakage is often a problem during the first months of nursing, particularly in the breast not being used at the moment. You may also find the cup useful in holding the bra away from sore nipples so that air can circulate. Can be sterilized. Order from:
The Netsy Co. (Marianne Alstrom), 34 Sunrise Ave., Mill Valley, CA 94941 ($7.95 a pair)

Pads for Absorbing Milk Leakage

Happy Family Products carries both disposable and washable bra pads. The contoured paper pads have no irritating vinyls or plastics. Each pad has three layers and is diamond quilted for absorbency. Comfy-Dry pads are used for the same purpose as the disposable paper pads, but they are made of washable fabric quilting and can be machine-washed. (Not pictured.) Order from:
Happy Family Products, 1252 S. La Cienega Blvd., Los Angeles, CA 90035 (Disposable pads, $2.00 for a box of 48; fabric pads, $2.50 a pair)

Nursing Bras

Nursing moms no longer have to wear those dumpy pointed cups of the fifties! Montgomery Ward and Sears have fine collections of modern nursing bras with gently rounded cups. Some have fasteners that can be released with one hand — useful when you've got a hungry baby in your arms! Another model adjusts with hooks to several sizes, so that it can be adapted to breast-size changes during pregnancy and lactation. Your cup size during the last months of pregnancy should be a fairly accurate measure of how large a bra to buy. Bra extenders, which fasten easily onto back hooks, are handy helps for adapting bras that become too tight around your chest. Look for them in notions departments. You may find unfastening regular bras in the back for nursing or stretching spandex-type bras up over your breast to be more convenient and less cumbersome for nursing than unfastening and pulling down nursing flaps. Be careful, though, that your bra doesn't interfere with the flow of milk from the outer edges of the breast down to the nipple.

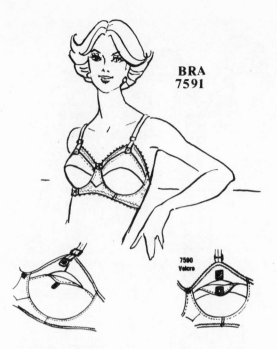

BRA
7591

7590
Velcro

Fancee Free Bras

The modern bra models shown are made of nylon tricot and have a choice of a velcro or bonnie clasp closure. The bras are available in either beige or white. Order from:
Fancee Free, 6609 Olive Blvd., St. Louis, MO 63130 ($8.50 + $1.50 postage and handling)

Breast Milking and Feeding Unit

This simple suction breast pump works with a gentle, piston-like motion. The milk remains in the collection unit, which can then be used as a feeding bottle. The entire unit can be sterilized. Included is a practical instruction brochure of techniques for gathering milk for special situations, such as hospitalization or work-day absences. Write for the catalogue of baby products:
Happy Family Products, 1252 S. La Cienega Blvd., Los Angeles, CA 90035 (Approx. $21.50)

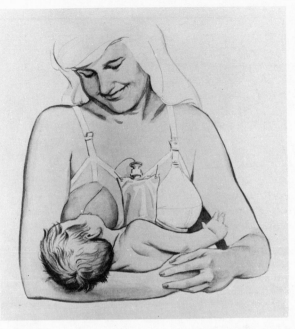

Lact-Aid

A feeding device composed of a plastic bag and a tiny tube to be used in carrying supplemental formula, or donor human milk, to a baby at the same time that she's suckling on her mother's breast. Its purpose is to help the mother in getting adequate stimulation for milk production while the Lact-Aid simultaneously provides nourishment. It's useful to mothers who find it necessary to reinitiate breastfeeding because their infants are allergic to milks other than breastmilk, or mothers wishing to nurse adopted babies. (Write Mrs. Jimmie Lynne Avery at the address below for more information on this topic.) You shouldn't really need one if you plan to breastfeed your baby from birth.
Resources in Human Nurturing, Int'l., P.O. Box 6861, Denver, CO 80206 ($17.00)

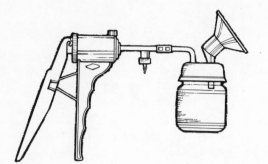

Loyd-B Pump

Breast pumps are useful when a mother and baby are separated from each other. If milk is allowed to build up in the breasts from not being nursed for a day or so, it's painful and signals the body to stop making milk. Breastmilk, gathered under sterile conditions, can be saved and given to Baby later or frozen for up to two years. (For more information on human milk banks, see *Nursing Your Baby* by Karen Pryor.) The Loyd-B Pump consists of a glass bottle connected to the breast at one end by a shield and with a hand-grip at the other end for making a vacuum. The milk flows downward into the collection bottle. The pump is nonelectric, light-weight, and can be sterilized. Before you purchase a pump, check to see if your local La Leche League can lend you one. If not, order from:
LOPUCO, 6117 Parkway Dr., West Laurel, MD 20810 ($35.00 + $2.00 postage)

Nursing Fashions

Bright, casual outfits for nursing Moms. These tops have velcro-fastened flaps for easy access and closure. Style #1 is white eyelet cotton/polyester; #2 is cotton/polyester with printed sleeves. Both tops come in bust sizes 32, 34, 36, 38, and 40. The dress, #3, is predominantly blue and white and comes in sizes small, medium, and large. Allow 2 to 3 weeks for delivery. Order from:
Baby Love, P.O. Box 127, Laguna Beach, CA 92652 (#1, $19.95 + $1.25 postage and handling; #2, $14.95 + $1.25 postage and handling; #3, $29.95 + $1.75 postage and handling. California residents add tax)

Nursing Gown *(left)*

The nylon tricot gown (#5006) has a hidden front opening for ease in nursing. The Cover Up (#5016) is designed to coordinate with the gown and features a side pocket and buttoning front. Both come in beige, blue, yellow, and pink; sizes S, M, L (gown also in XS) are available. Write for a brochure of nursing bras and fashions:
Mary Jane Co., 4033 Sunset Blvd., Hollywood, CA 90029 (#5006, $13.50; #5016, $19.50)

PUBLICATIONS OF INTEREST

All of the following publications can be ordered from: *La Leche League International, Inc., 9616 Minneapolis Ave., Franklin Park, IL 60131. (Also ask for their list of literature and recommended books.)*

"Breastfeeding and Working?"
Mary Anne Cahill
(50¢)
The League feels that the mother should spend the first months of baby life at home with Baby. (I must say that I agree.) Nonetheless, if a mother has no alternative, this brochure gives some ideas on how to breastfeed and hold a job at the same time — perhaps through part-time work arrangements. Includes suggestions on choosing a sitter and planning the day.

La Leche League News
($2.75 per year)
An enjoyable little bimonthly magazine for breastfeeding mothers. Includes success stories, useful child-care hints, and the latest research on breastfeeding.

"Management of Successful Lactation"
M. Newton, N. R. Newton, and R. M. Applebaum
($1.00)
A fifty-page reprint from *Child and Family* magazine that serves as a good reference for the technical aspects of breastfeeding. Written by two physicians and a scientist-mother.

Nursing Your Baby
Karen Pryor
($1.95, Pocket Books paperback)
The best book available, in my opinion, for guiding the beginning mother through the nursing experience. Mrs. Pryor, an experienced breastfeeding mother, combines clear scientific information with practical baby-management hints.

The Womanly Art of Breastfeeding
($3.50, paperback)
The La Leche League's own manual. Provides very practical, simple advice. Overlook the chapter "The Father's Role," which belongs in the Victorian era.

Books available from bookstores or by mail order:

Heartstart! A Practical Guide to an Optimum Breastfeeding Experience
Ilene S. Rice
2392 Nancy Place, St. Paul, MN 55113 ($3.25)
A small guide, published by its author, that is a great "first aid" handbook for breastfeeding. Deals with how to position the baby, how to express milk, and how to deal with breast engorgement.

A Loving Start
Saul Blatman, M.D.
Research Media, Inc., 96 Mt. Auburn St., Cambridge, MA 02138 ($6.25 each volume)
A three-book series including: *Breastfeeding — Getting Ready* (#211230); *Breastfeeding — Now Your Baby Is Here* (#211231); and *Bottle Feeding* (#211232). The volumes on breastfeeding give clear, practical how-to instructions. These books are easy to read and have many good photographs.

Preparation for Breast Feeding
Donna Ewy and Rodger Ewy
Doubleday & Co., 277 Park Ave., NYC 10017 ($2.95, paperback)
An excellent and practical handbook that deals realistically with the joys and difficulties of nursing. Includes topics such as the importance of the father's support, dealing with a colicky baby, treating sore nipples, and many other aspects of breastfeeding.

You Can Breastfeed Your Baby
Dorothy Patricia Brewster
Rodale Press, Rodor & Co., P.O. Box 2003, Palos Verdes Peninsula, CA 90274 ($11.95, paperback)
A large volume (624 pages) covering a vast range of breastfeeding information, including case studies of mothers who have breastfed babies afflicted by Down's syndrome; adopted babies; and twins. Discusses what to do about a baby who refuses to nurse, how to deal with sickness and hospitalization, and how to travel with a nursing baby. A virtual encyclopedia!

Note: Not all manufacturers and publishers will accept single orders for a product or book. Always write them first, before sending money, to be certain that they will accept your order and make sure that you have the most recent price, including shipping and handling charges.

A DANGEROUS OLDER CAR SEAT

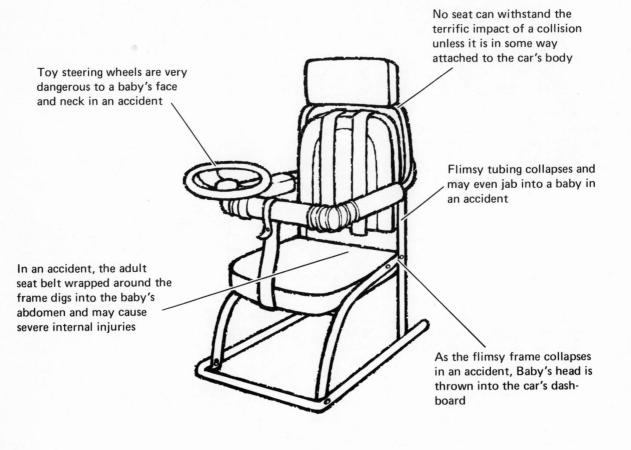

Toy steering wheels are very dangerous to a baby's face and neck in an accident

No seat can withstand the terrific impact of a collision unless it is in some way attached to the car's body

Flimsy tubing collapses and may even jab into a baby in an accident

In an accident, the adult seat belt wrapped around the frame digs into the baby's abdomen and may cause severe internal injuries

As the flimsy frame collapses in an accident, Baby's head is thrown into the car's dashboard

Car and Bicycle Seats

The National Safety Council reports that over 1800 babies and children under the age of four are killed in automobile accidents each year. An accident that involves a sudden stop, even when the car is going slowly, can throw a baby into the car's instrument panel or other hard objects and cause severe injury, particularly to his head. If a baby is thrown out of his parent's arms, or a car bed or seat, he continues to travel at the car's speed seconds after the car has stopped. A baby held in the front-seat passenger's arms occupies what safety experts call the "death seat." It's impossible to brace against the impact of a sudden stop in time to protect Baby.

The Consumer's Union of the United States has run extensive tests on infant's and children's safety seats in order to determine how they would perform under the impact of 30 mph front, rear, and side collisions. The popular aluminum tubular seats collapsed, throwing a dummy child's head into the instrument panel with sufficient force to kill a real child immediately. The force of the adult seat belt wrapped around the carrier would have most likely caused severe abdominal injuries. **Warning: Do not use aluminum-framed car seats.**

After years of delay, the U.S. Department of Transportation, the National Highway Traffic Safety Administration, has finally issued a revised set of car-seat and car-bed regulations, Standard 213-80, which is slated to go into effect May 1, 1980. After that time, only dynamically tested car seats and car beds are to be sold in the United States.

Dynamic testing means that car restraints must undergo simulated crashes using a carefully weighted dummy representing a six-month-old infant and another representing a three-year-old child. In a head-on crash at 30 mph the car seat or car bed is required to hold together without breaking, and it must limit the amount of movement made by the occupant's body, head, and knees. In this way, babies and children are protected from injuries caused by the restraint and also from injuries caused by ramming into the interior of the car.

Other parts of Standard 213-80 deal with the durability of restraint materials, the amount of force that should be necessary to release the belts, and stipulations for clearly worded owner's instructions.

At the present time, nearly all car restraints passing dynamic tests make use of a "tether" strap, a belt in the upper rear of the car seat that must be bolted to the car's frame as directed by the manufacturer. Studies have shown that in more than half the cases examined, parents are not attaching the tether as directed. If the tether is not used correctly, these car seats lose most of their protection value. **Warning: Be sure to use the car seat's rear tether strap as directed by the manufacturer.**

The sturdy, safe, new car seats are expensive, so be prepared to spend as much as $50.00. A good way to justify the expense is to realize that you would probably pay $150.00 for an optional radio or for air conditioning and other features in a new car. Certainly $50.00 isn't much, when you consider the protection the seat will give your little one for four years. Think of it as an insurance policy!

Some features to look for when shopping for a car seat:

● The best investment is a single seat that adapts to both infant and toddler positions.

● Choose a seat that sits high enough for a toddler to see out the window. (This suggestion comes from hundreds of parents I have interviewed.)

● For summer comfort, choose a model that has a non-shiny upholstery.

● Check to see that the seat's straps are easy to adjust.

• The seat should be semi-reclining in the infant position, so that Baby doesn't slump over.

• Try the latches to make sure that you can operate them with relative ease. (Federal regulations require that latches be relatively difficult to open, to prevent toddlers from releasing themselves.)

• If you have a small car, be sure that the child's seat is narrow enough to fit in your back seat, particularly if the adult belt must encircle the seat's shield.

RECOMMENDED CAR SEATS

The following seats have been given very high ratings by parents of babies and toddlers. They represent the best in design currently available on the market.

General Motors Infant Love Seat
Baby faces to the rear in this molded plastic bucket with foam padding. Belts secure his shoulders and the adult safety belt passes through side holes to hold the carrier firmly to the car's seat. Dynamically tested. Excellent for use at home as an infant seat, but be sure to use as directed. With some of the older models, babies have been injured by catching their necks on the openings on each side of the seat where the adult seat belt passes across the baby seat. A modification kit for these models is available free from G.M. at the address below.
G.M. Love Seats, 400 Renaissance Center, Suite 1200, Detroit, MI 48243 (Approx. $25.00)

General Motors Child Love Seat
A padded, molded plastic seat that sits high enough for a child to look out at passing scenery. Dynamically tested. Designed for children weighing from 20 to 40 lbs. Shoulder and over-the-leg belts — that are awkward to adjust and fasten — hold the child in place. The top of the carrier should be bolted to the car frame or hooked to a rear seat belt when in the front seat (see the manufacturer's instructions). An adult seat belt secures the carrier to the car. A yard sale bargain. Also available from G.M. dealers and baby departments in stores. Manufactured by:
G.M. Love Seats, 400 Renaissance Center, Suite 1200, Detroit, MI 48243 (Approx. $45.00)

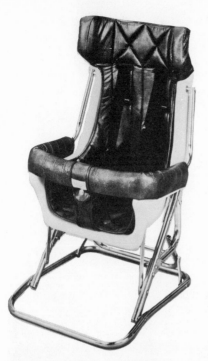

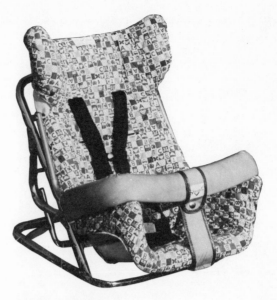

"Strolee" Seat Liner

An absorbent quilted cotton/polyester liner helps make the "Strolee" seat more comfortable on hot summer days. (A similar cover is manufactured by "Strolee.") Available in bright prints. Order from:
Lil' Lovins', P.O. Box 3114, Nashua, NH 03061 ($12.95 + $1.00 postage and handling)

"Strolee" Wee Care Car Seat

A dynamically tested seat, this restraint has become the favorite of many parents. It sits up high, allowing tots to watch the passing scenery. The seat adjusts for use both by infants in a rear-facing position in the front seat and by upright tots in the back seat. For maximum safety, anchor the rear tether strap as directed and do not rely on the front arm bar as a restraint. The firmly fastened harness system on the seat provides its restraining power. Available in shiny vinyl or a more comfortable leather-look finish. Manufactured by: *"Strolee" of California, 19067 South Reyes Ave., Compton, CA 90221 (Approx. $45.00)*

Peterson 78 Safe-T-Seat *(right)*

This dynamically tested, well-designed seat can be used both for rear-facing babies in the front seat and for toddlers in an upright position in the rear seat of the car. The seat reclines at a number of angles, although many safety experts feel that such seats are safer in an erect position. For maximum safety a tether strap at the upper rear of the seat must be fastened to the car frame, as directed by the manufacturer. Features that make this seat worth its higher price: soft, less sticky-when-hot upholstery in grey, tan, or beige; the high stance of the seat, which allows for tot viewing; and the wideness of the seat, which accommodates tots in winter garb. Remember that the front bar of the seat is merely decorative and has no restraining value of its own. Latch Baby in securely with the harness belts provided. Manufactured by:
Peterson Baby Products, 4421 Riverside Dr., Suite 212, Toluca Lake, CA 91505 (Approx. $60.00)

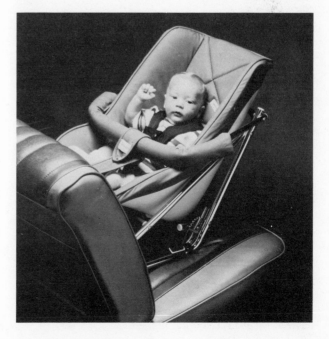

CONSUMER INFORMATION

The following organizations provide information on the selection of car restraints for babies and children:

ACTION FOR CHILD TRANSPORTATION SAFETY, INC.

P.O. Box 266, Bothell, WA 98011
Inexpensive brochures plus an excellent film showing dynamic tests in progress.

CONSUMERS UNION

256 Washington St., Mt. Vernon, NY 10550
Look in back issues of *Consumer Reports* for reviews of car seats.

INSURANCE INSTITUTE FOR HIGHWAY SAFETY

Watergate 600, Washington, DC 20037
Reprints of technical studies on car seat usage by parents.

PHYSICIANS FOR AUTO SAFETY

50 Union Ave., Irvington, NJ 07111
Brochures and film available.

DEPARTMENT OF TRANSPORTATION, NATIONAL HIGHWAY TRAFFIC SAFETY ADMINISTRATION

400 7th St., S.W. (NAD–42), Washington, DC 20590
Public information brochures on car seat selection; also, copies of car seat regulations. For the latest information on car seat safety, send for a free copy of *The Early Rider Fact Book*.

BICYCLE SEATS

Small children can be injured on their parents' bicycles because of poorly designed bicycle seats. The most frequent injury among children is to catch a heel in the wheel spokes, causing a severe wound that takes a long time to heal. An adequate bicycle seat should offer good heel and leg protection as well as sturdy seat belts for securing the child in the seat.

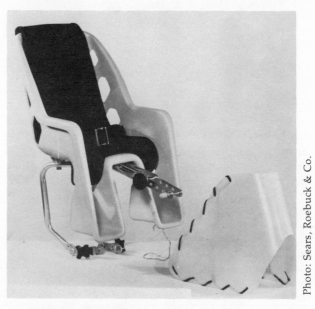

Photo: Sears, Roebuck & Co.

Sears Best Bicycle Carrier
This bright yellow jockey-styled carrier centers the young child's weight over the bicycle's rear wheel. Once the seat is installed it can be removed from the bicycle frame by unscrewing three knobs. Leg wells on the high-backed seat and a spoke guard protect feet from injury. Order from your local Sears. Headquarters: *Sears, Roebuck & Co., Sears Tower, Chicago, IL 60684 (Approx. $20.00)*

Note: Not all manufacturers and publishers will accept single orders for a product or book. Always write them first, before sending money, to be certain that they will accept your order and make sure that you have the most recent price, including shipping and handling charges.

Carriages

Buy yourself a carriage only if your neighborhood is suitable! Do you have paved sidewalks and lots of strolling space? Then consider one. But if there are a lot of curbs and bumps to negotiate, a carriage may prove to be more trouble than it's worth. If you're a city dweller, or an apartment resident, then a baby carriage is going to present problems. Carriages are bulky, hard to manage over curbs, and difficult to fold and store. Suburban mothers spend a great deal of time running errands in the car, and you can imagine the inconvenience of having to collapse the carriage, put it in the trunk, drive to the shopping center, open the carriage, and start again — only to repeat the process for the return home. Also, carriages are an expensive investment for most couples, considering the relatively short time that Baby is content to recline in one. On the other hand, mothers who live in really cold climates like the protection that a carriage affords from gusty winds. Carriages are handy, too, for poolside use in summer when covered with mosquito netting.

If you do want a carriage, consider buying a used one and making it Baby's first bed as well. Inside the house, the carriage can be conveniently rolled from room to room. The gentle rocking motion and the dark, enclosed feeling of the carriage help newborns to feel quite secure.

Here are the features to look for when purchasing a carriage:
• Check to see that the carriage is the right height and weight for you — not so low that it tips, nor too heavy for negotiating curbs and steps.
• Make sure that you can see over the hood when it's up.
• Check to see that the brakes hold securely and that they are easy to operate, preferably from the rear. Four-wheel brakes are superior to two-wheel.

Photo: Perego/Barclay Co.

• Check the interior — all metal ribs should be covered and, preferably, padded.
• Is the suspension system adequate for absorbing bumps and knocks?
• Is the carriage easy to collapse and reopen? Is there a secure safety-catch system to prevent accidental collapsing?
• Make sure there are no flimsy ornamental parts or sharp, protruding edges that might later injure an exploring baby and no dangerous "X" joints, which could entrap small fingers.

Convertible carriages have a removable body that can be used as a bed and can later be adapted for use as a stroller. They're good buys if the parts fasten very securely to the carriage frame and if the stroller seems comfortable and well designed.

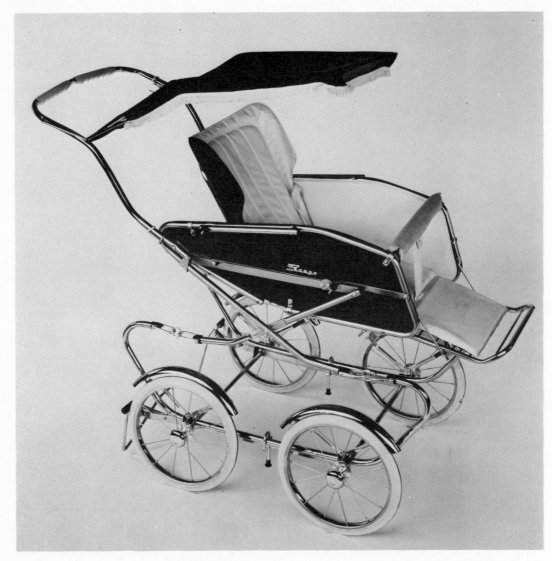

Photo: Perego/Barclay Co.

CARRIAGE ACCESSORIES

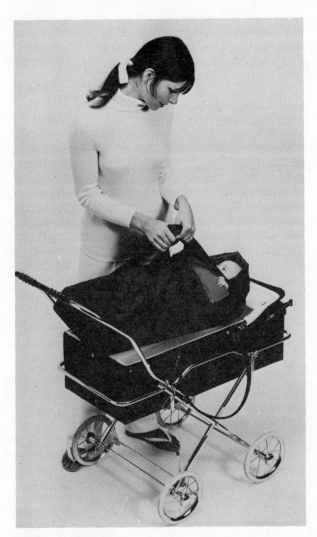

Carriage Bag
A heavy-duty vinyl-coated fabric bag that hooks onto the handlebar of a carriage. It has two roomy outer pockets with zipper closings. Colors: red, navy, green, black, white, or light blue. A Baby Carriage Hospital also carries accessories and repair parts for carriages and strollers. For their free catalogue, write:
A Baby Carriage Hospital, 5935 W. Irving Park Rd., Chicago, IL 60634 ($16.95 + $2.00 postage and handling)

> **Note:** Not all manufacturers and publishers will accept single orders for a product or book. Always write them first, before sending money, to be certain that they will accept your order and make sure that you have the most recent price, including shipping and handling charges.

Mothercare Cocoon
A washable zip-up carry-cot (as the English call it) made of warm, quilted fabric. For use with very young babies. Can be placed directly into the carriage. Navy with red interior. Order from:
Mothercare-by-Mail, 196 Quaker Bridge Mall, U.S. Rt. 1 and Quaker Bridge Rd., Lawrenceville, NJ 08648 (Approx. $18.00)

Chairs for Feeding and Carrying Baby

BABY CHAIRS

Baby chairs are generally made of molded plastic with a plastic pad or of a pressed wood covered in plastic. Baby can sit in several positions, from reclining to almost erect. The advantage of a baby chair is that Baby can view the world around him rather than having to stare at the ceiling as he would in a bassinet. Because of the erect position they put a baby in, baby chairs also have been found helpful in treating babies with digestive problems, frequent vomiting, or nasal congestion. Some mothers like to use them when feeding a young baby who is unable to sit up in a highchair, or to put them in grocery carts while shopping.

Baby chairs, like every other device that holds or restrains a baby, must be used with caution and common sense. The Consumer Product Safety Commission estimates that in 1972 there occured 1,000 infant-seat-related injuries serious enough to require emergency-room treatment. Most were head injuries and resulted from falls from high places. A fall while strapped in a baby chair can hurt a baby more than it would if he were free to use his natural reflexes to protect himself.

Some child-care experts dislike the infant seat because it removes the baby from the warmth and protection of his mother's arms. Physical contact and cuddling are extremely important to a baby's sense of well-being. Also, if a mother carrying a baby in an infant seat falls, she is more likely to throw the baby, seat and all, away from her, but if she's carrying the baby in her arms, she is more likely to protect him instinctively during the fall.

Some mothers have found that continual use of the chair has caused their babies' muscular development to progress more slowly. The baby chair prevents the baby from reaching out, touching objects, holding his head up, and doing the other motions necessary for strengthening his muscles.

A final criticism of the infant seat is that some models keep the baby's legs close together. Babies naturally hold their legs widely separated, in a froglike position. It is thought that the leg spread helps to direct the thigh bone into the hip while the hip socket is being formed.

Here are some suggestions as to what to look for when purchasing an infant chair:

• The base of the chair should be wider than the seat itself in order to provide maximum security. Test the chair with your hand. Does it tip over easily?
• Check the back of the chair to see that the seat adjustment mechanisms hold securely in each position. Is there a danger that the seat might collapse under the weight of a bouncing baby? (The cheaper, flimsier models are more likely to tear or give way.)
• Are there any sharp edges or parts that could hurt a baby if he fell out of the seat, or into the seat base from outside? Infant chairs with protruding metal rockers are unsafe.
• Does the chair base have a nonslip surface?
• Check to see that the chair has sturdy safety straps with a firmly holding buckle and a crotch strap so that Baby can't slide out feet first.

If you decide to purchase and use an infant chair, follow these simple rules:

• Use the infant seat sparingly — only in temporary situations. *Never use it as a baby-sitter.*
• Never use an infant seat as a car seat. It would be dangerous in the event of an accident.
• Always use the seat's safety straps to keep Baby from toppling out.
• Never leave a baby unattended in an infant seat. The

possibilities of injury from falls or getting caught in the straps are numerous.

• Never put a seat high up on a smooth surface, such as a table top, where Baby's motion could propel the seat off the side. It's best to keep the seat on the floor, where the baby won't be hurt if he should manage to flip the seat over.

• Be careful when using an infant seat in a stroller or grocery cart. For example, some babies have been injured toppling out of the back of a stroller in the infant seat when their mothers tilted the stroller to negotiate a curb. Other babies have been injured when brothers and sisters have overturned shopping carts, baby and all.

INFANT CHAIRS AND ACCESSORIES

Wink-N-Wake
A wide-based seat that offers maximum stability. The plastic quilting is foam-padded. The back can be adjusted into a number of positions with a safety lock. Manufactured by:
Kantwet, Questor Juvenile Furniture Division, 771 N. Freedom St., Ravenna, OH 44266 (Approx. $20.00)

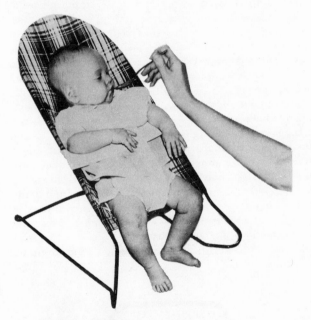

Comfy-Babe Chair
A spring-action fabric chair that allows the tiniest baby to set off a gentle rocking merely by raising and lowering an arm or a leg. The brightly patterned cotton back can be removed for washing. A wide, adjustable belt keeps the baby in. Order from:
The Comfy-Babe Co., P.O. Box 326, Downers Grove, IL 60515 ($15.00)

Wooden Seat Pattern
You can make a sturdy seat for Baby! The seat is traced directly onto the wood for easy construction, and the pattern for the interior padding is included. (*Not safe for use as a car seat.*) Order the #177 Tot Toter pattern from:
U-Bild Enterprises, P.O. Box 2383, Van Nuys, CA 91409 ($1.00)

Bouncinette

Baby can make this seat jiggle with a move of the hand or foot. It's manufactured in Australia and is engineered for balance, with a washable mesh cover and a sturdy steel frame. Air circulates freely, which is a plus for summer use. (Booties and butterflies are also available from the free, full-color catalogue of baby products.) Order from:

Children's Design Center, 29 Excelsior Springs Ave., Saratoga Springs, NY 12866 ($32.00 + $2.00 postage and handling)

Pedestal Seat

Imported from Holland, this wide-based seat has a safety belt and a between-the-legs strap; it adjusts from upright to reclining positions. This seat comes in brown with a bright orange cushion or in yellow with a brown cushion. Order from:

Children's Design Center, 29 Excelsior Springs Ave., Saratoga Springs, NY 12866 ($35.00 + $2.00 postage and handling)

HIGHCHAIRS

The highchair is a dangerous household device that has been responsible for the deaths of some babies and children. Some have fatally injured their heads when falling; others have strangled or broken their necks while entrapped under the chair's tray. The U.S. Product Safety Commission estimates that there are approximately 7,000 highchair-related injuries treated in hospital emergency rooms per year. Most of these accidents involve babies and children under four.

A typical example of what happens to babies is that of a seven-month-old boy who was treated for a deep cut across his nose and cheek. His mother had placed him in the highchair and put the tray on. The tray, which hadn't locked securely, gave way, and the baby fell to the floor, striking the tray's upturned locking device, which had sharp edges. Other babies stand up and then fall from the chair, some onto hot burners, or they pull the chair over on themselves from outside of it; and sometimes a collapsible chair gives way — perhaps amputating a finger in a dangerous metal "X" joint.

A standard of safety features for highchairs has recently been adopted for the industry by highchair manufacturers. The standard includes locking devices to prevent chairs from collapsing with children in them, an effective restraining system to prevent falls, a restriction against scissoring actions in collapsible chairs, and the removal of sharp edges and openings that might injure a baby's hands or fingers. (A detailed statement of the standard may be ordered for $1.75 from: Sales/Service Department of the American Society for Testing and Materials, 1916 Race Street, Philadelphia, PA 19103.) The catch is that no manufacturer *has* to conform to the standard; it is voluntary.

Look for this certification mark when shopping for a highchair:

Here are the features to look for when choosing a highchair:

• The legs should have a wide stance for tip-proof stability.
• The tray should lock firmly into place, and you should be able to operate the lock easily without having to bend down to look.
• There should be a sturdy restraining system, including waist and crotch belts.
• The chair should have locks to prevent accidental collapse.

It's also wise to follow these simple suggestions when using a highchair:

• Never allow a baby or child to stand in a chair.
• For added safety, use a halter-type strap on the shoulders (see ''Safety Harnesses,'' p. 83), to insure that Baby can't fall out.
• Don't depend on the tray to hold Baby in, and always double-check to be sure that the tray is properly locked in place.

A POORLY DESIGNED HIGHCHAIR

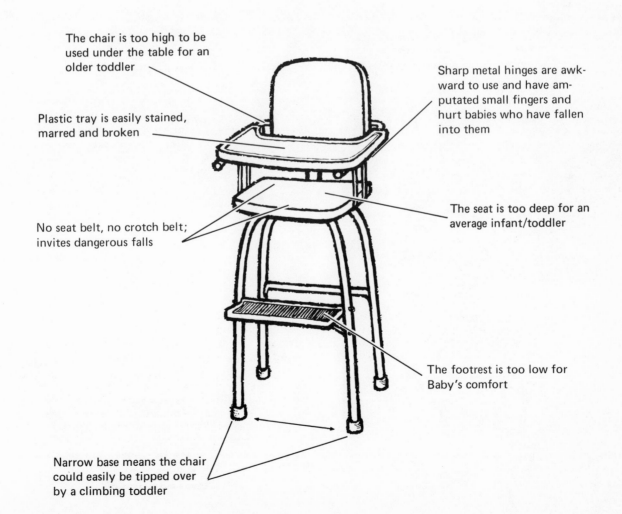

The chair is too high to be used under the table for an older toddler

Plastic tray is easily stained, marred and broken

No seat belt, no crotch belt; invites dangerous falls

Narrow base means the chair could easily be tipped over by a climbing toddler

Sharp metal hinges are awkward to use and have amputated small fingers and hurt babies who have fallen into them

The seat is too deep for an average infant/toddler

The footrest is too low for Baby's comfort

Grandpa's Chair

Grandpa makes this tyke's chair of pegs and glue with no metal, paint, or varnish. The chair is low; the tray is removable and has a wooden peg lock. What could be safer? Order from:
Grandpa's Wooden Toys, Rt. 9, Box 453, Florence, AL 35630 ($15.00 + shipping; U.S. orders only.)

"Strolee" Classic Highchair

Parents have given this chair a top rating. The extra-large rimmed tray helps prevent spills. The thick vinyl-covered padding is comfortable and relatively easy to clean. The chair converts to a youth chair for use at the table. It can also be used as a kitchen chair by adults. Dual safety belts hold Baby at the waist and across the legs to prevent slipping out or standing. Chair collapses for storage. Manufactured by:
"Strolee" of California, 19067 S. Reyes Ave., Compton, CA 90221 (Approx. $50.00)

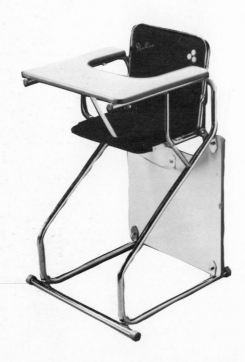

High and Low Chair *(left)*

Manufactured by Silver Cross, England's famous baby carriage company, this chair is, in its upright position, a standard highchair. Horizontally, it is a safe, low feeding table. Both positions have a between-the-legs belt. (Use a harness for extra safety in the upright position.) The movable seat is the secret to the ingenious design. The seat is a stain-resistant chocolate brown wide-wale corduroy. The laminated trays are not removable. Order from:
Children's Design Center, 29 Excelsior Springs Ave., Saratoga Springs, NY 12866 ($85.00 freight collect)

Hokus Pokus Chair

This Swedish chair has been given the highest recommendation by the Swedish consumer's bureau because of its strength, stability, and usefulness. The chair is made of molded plastic with rounded edges. In the upright position, it's used at the family table for feeding. Lying face up, it's a rocking chair and make-believe car with a tot-sized steering wheel. What a remarkable design! Available in blue, yellow, red, or white. For further information, contact:

Hokus Pokus America, P.O. Box 376, Southhampton, PA 18966 ($70.00 + $4.00 postage and handling)

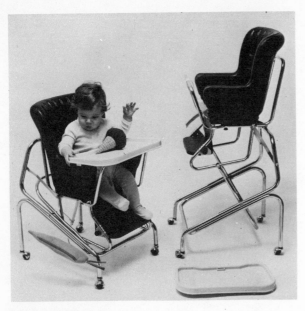

Brevi Highchair

A functional highchair designed by a pediatrician for safety, comfort, and practicality. The chrome frame adjusts from highchair to low feeding-table position. The footrest raises or lowers for good leg support. The dishwashable tray can be adjusted to two positions. The seat is deeply cushioned and comes in navy or brown. Order from:
Children's Design Center, 29 Excelsior Springs Ave., Saratoga Springs, NY 12866 ($79.00 + $6.00 shipping)

Wooden Highchair (Model 7-819)

A traditional highchair with rounded, smooth bars to make cleaning easier. It has widely spaced legs for stability and an adjustable, removable tray. The safety belt system fits around the baby's waist, and there's also a strap for between the legs. Manufactured by:
Hedstrom Co., Bedford, PA 15522 (Approx. $60.00)

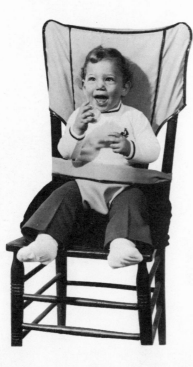

Ti-Chair *(left)*

A fabric chair restraint that lets you feed Baby with no danger of falls when visiting or in restaurants. The pillowcase design slips over the back of a standard chair and then ties around Baby's waist. The seat is constructed with a soft foam inner cushion. Handwashable polyester/cotton blue denim with red vinyl edging. Order from:
Young Royalty, Inc., 915 West 30th St., NYC 10001 ($9.95)

Tripp Trapp Chair
A marvelous chair that allows the footrest and seat levels to be adjusted to accommodate a baby's growth. It is intended for use at the family table and does not have a tray. The curved wood guardrail is optional and has a between-the-legs leather strap, which is valuable for restraint. Colors: natural, beech, red, or dark brown. Order from:
Children's Design Center, 29 Excelsior Springs Ave., Saratoga Springs, NY 12866 (Chair, $64.00; guardrail, $13.00 plus $6.00 shipping)

Note: Not all manufacturers and publishers will accept single orders for a product or book. Always write them first, before sending money, to be certain that they will accept your order and make sure that you have the most recent price, including shipping and handling charges.

FEEDING TABLES

A feeding table has the following advantages:
• It's lower to the ground — so falls, if they occur, are less likely to cause serious injury.
• There is no removable tray. The tray may be dangerous in two ways: it may give way, causing an unrestrained baby to fall to the floor, if it is not properly latched; and it may have sharp, pinching devices that can injure a baby's fingers or cause more serious injury in the case of a fall.
• It is more stable — in fact, it's virtually tip-proof.
• It can be rolled under the regular dining room table when not in use.
• It's adaptable for later use as a play table for arts and crafts.

The major disadvantage with feeding tables is that it is difficult to put Baby in and take him out of the chair. Some babies have had their legs bruised when they were lifted from the table while their legs were trapped underneath.

Here's what to look for when buying a feeding table:
• Shake the standing table to see how sturdy it is.
• Look at the adjustment mechanism for the seat. Does it seem strong and easy to operate?
• How secure is the locking mechanism for the legs?
• Is there a sturdy safety belt that also goes between the legs to prevent sliding under the table?
• How durable is the footrest? Some feeding tables have shoddy, stapled footrests that break off easily.

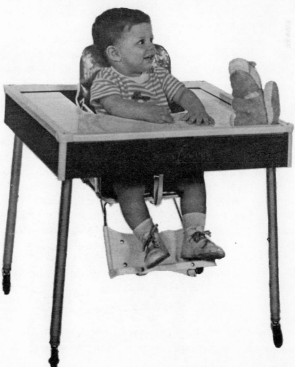

Photo: Baby-Tenda Corp.

Clothes

It's a problem to know how much and what kind of clothing to buy before the baby comes. Really, there's no rush to have Baby's wardrobe complete before she is born — you can always manage a trip to the store afterwards to pick up the things you need. How many clothes you should buy depends on how accessible laundry facilities are. If you have a washing machine and dryer at home, you can make do with less clothing than you need if you had to go to a laundromat.

You can figure on Baby using about three or four cotton-knit shirts a day. This may seem like a lot, but babies spit up frequently and shirts get wet from diapers. The best choice is the tie-on shirt because it adjusts better than snap-tabbed shirts do as Baby grows. It's also more comfortable for Baby to lie on. Pullover shirts would be a poor choice — both babies and tots hate having clothing pulled over their heads! It's best to buy shirts in the six-month size, except for one or two small, footed sleepers for going outside.

All a new baby needs to wear indoors is a cotton shirt and diapers. This way her arms and legs get the touching and rubbing she needs for stimulation. Her hands and feet are naturally colder than the rest of her body; it's no sign that she should be completely covered. Receiving blankets are always handy during the first months to wrap the baby lightly when it seems cool. Plan on Baby's using two or three of these a day. If Baby seems fretful, you might try wrapping her more firmly in the blanket — sometimes a baby can be soothed by being temporarily swaddled. Normally, though, she should be allowed complete freedom to move and kick.

A thoughtful Grandma will buy Baby everyday clothes that are comfortable and easily laundered, rather than ornate laces and dresses, which often have scratchy, uncomfortable seams. Dresses are particularly unsuitable for the baby who is trying to crawl. Then too, a dress may be worn only once or twice before it's outgrown or out of season, whereas the same money might be more wisely invested in blankets, shirts, and everyday things that will remain useful longer.

Most of the ornate sweaters, hats, and booties that are given as shower gifts are poor choices for tiny babies. If a sweater isn't tightly knit, Baby will get her fingers entangled in the threads. Hats are quite bothersome to Baby because by touching her face they set off the rooting reflex, making her turn left and right in search of food. Newborns also dislike booties and quickly kick them off by pushing one foot against the other.

Footed stretch sleepers are convenient and popular, but they shouldn't be Baby's habitual dress, because they block off sensations in her arms and feet. They are best used for going outdoors. You'll find three or four of them to be all you need. Be careful not to use a stretch suit after it begins to fit tightly. Inspect the inside of the footed part after each washing and clip all of the small strings that might become entangled in Baby's toes and constrict them. A bunting (a zip-up sack with arms in it) is handy for quick dressing when you're going outside, but in order not to swallow Baby up, it must be in a small size.

When Baby begins to pull up on furniture and to crawl, her clothing needs will change radically. It's time to buy long pants that will protect Baby's legs from knee burn on carpets and later from the knocks and bumps of repeated falls. Overalls that button at the shoulder and have snaps at the crotch are the most convenient pants to use. One mother I know made her son several pairs of these overalls from an easy McCall's sewing pattern, in a quilted fabric — a fine cushion against bruising falls!

In summer, it's important to keep Baby's head cov-

GUIDE TO BUYING BABY CLOTHES

AGE (MONTHS)	SMALL BABY	AVERAGE BABY	BIG BABY	BEST BUYS
up to 3	3 mos. size *(up to 13 lbs.; 21–23")*	3 mos. size *(up to 13 lbs.; 21–23")*	6 mos. size *(14–18 lbs.; 24–26")*	*Cotton-knit shirts with tie or snap fasteners* *Prefolded diapers* *Receiving blankets* *Footed sleepers* *Nightgowns*
3–6	3 mos. size *(up to 13 lbs.; 21–23")*	6 mos. size *(14–18 lbs.; 24–26")*	12 mos. size *(19–22 lbs.; 26–28")*	*Pull-on plastic pants* *Zip-up buntings*
6–9	6 mos. size *(14–18 lbs.; 24–26")*	12 mos. size *(19–22 lbs.; 26–28")*	18 mos. size *(23–26 lbs.; 28–30")*	*Bright cotton-knit shirts, short- or long-sleeved, with buttons or snaps at the shoulders* *Washable sweaters* *Tie-on hat (knit for winter, brimmed for summer)*
9–12	6 mos. size *(14–18 lbs.; 24–26")*	12 mos. size *(19–22 lbs.; 26–28")*	18 mos. size *(23–26 lbs.; 28–30")*	*Button-on overalls with gripper crotch* *Hooded jacket* *Pull-on plastic pants*
12–18	12 mos. size *(19–22 lbs.; 26–28")*	18 mos. size *(23–26 lbs.; 28–30")*	24 mos. size *(27–29 lbs.; 30–32")*	*Raincoat and galoshes* *Pull-on pants with elastic waistband* *Swimsuit and sleeveless tank tops (for summer)*
18–24	18 mos. size *(23–26 lbs.; 28–30")*	24 mos. size *(27–29 lbs.; 30–32")*	24 mos. size *(27–29 lbs.; 30–32")*	*Mittens, sweaters, and other cold-weather clothes* *Extra-roomy training pants* *Winter coat*

ered and to be on guard against sunburn, which can happen very quickly in little ones. Some babies may get a mild form of sunstroke from playing in the bright, glaring sun without any protection. The night after they've been out, they get a sudden fever that disappears as quickly as it comes. It's best to put swing sets, sandboxes, and other play equipment in the shade. A tie-on brimmed hat is a good buy.

Here are some hints for buying clothes (See also "Shoes and Booties," pp. 86–87):

• Avoid clothes that have constricting elastic bands at the arms or ankles. (If unavoidable, any bands that leave marks on Baby's skin should be clipped with scissors.)

• Inspect the inside of dresses and shirts to see that the seams are soft and not scratchy. Check the legholes of plastic-lined pants to make sure they are soft and free from scratchy edges.

• Don't buy playsuits that have exposed metal zippers in the front. They can pinch Baby's skin.

• Be sure to buy clothes that will not fade and can be machine-washed and dried. Most sleepers and cotton-knit shirts and training pants shrink with washing; so buy a size or two too large to begin with.

• Avoid clothing that is difficult to put on and take off. The diaper area should be accessible without your having to remove the entire outfit.

As Baby begins to go outdoors, you may need to buy winter outerwear. Here are some suggestions for buying a coat or a snowsuit:

• Tie-on hoods are much easier to keep on a tot's head than hats, which most babies quickly pull off and dump. Hoods also offer protection for the ears and neck.

• A water-proof finish is practical for use in rain and snow.

• A zipper is easier to use than buttons.

• The garment should be warm, but not bulky. It shouldn't interfere with a toddler's arm movements. Some mothers so overdress their tots that the babies' arms are held in a stiff position. This is dangerous, for if the baby should fall, she couldn't use her natural bracing reflex.

You can get really good buys if you plan ahead and buy clothes for the coming year at the end of the season. Buy next year's coat, sweaters, and footed pajamas in January and February and summer playsuits and swimsuits in August and September. Use the shopping guide on the preceding page for help in predicting what size your baby will be next year.

HARD-TO-FIND CLOTHING

Illustration by Susan Hashim

Handkerchief Baby Bonnet
A christening bonnet made of fine handkerchief linen with French lace and white satin bows. Rip the four or five tackings and the cap opens up into a full-sized wedding handkerchief. If baby's name in filet is desired, add $1.95. Order from:
Villari Handkerchief Co., Room 516, 30 W. 54th St., NYC 10019 ($8.95)

Christening Gown Kit
An exquisite reproduction of a nineteenth-century christening gown and bonnet from the Brooklyn Museum. The kit contains lace, fabric, ribbons, and directions for sewing and embroidering. You can detail the gown and cap's handwork as intricately as you wish — but my advice is to start work on it while you're pregnant!
The Patchmakers, 920 Broadway, NYC 10010 ($16.95 plus $1.00 postage)

Finnwear Playsuit *(left)*
All-cotton construction means you don't have to worry about flammability! These marvelous suits come in brilliant red, yellow, and blue. They have zippers that go from the neck down the length of one leg. Sizes: 3 mos., 6 mos., 12 mos., and 18 mos. (The wooden play discs and lambskin are also available from the catalogue.) Order from:
Children's Design Center, 29 Excelsior Springs Ave., Saratoga Springs, NY 12866 ($12.00 plus $1.00 postage)

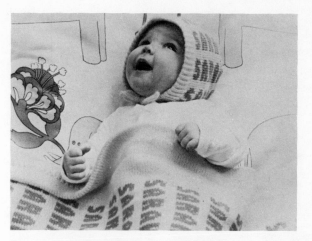

Personalized Baby Bonnet and Blanket
Your baby's name (7 letters or less) is knitted right into this bonnet and blanket set. The bonnet ties under the chin. There are twenty-one colors to choose from, including all of the bright primaries like yellow and red. Also available from this company is a toddler bonnet with a pompom on the back and a child's knit sweatshirt with a hood, in 12-, 18- and 24-month sizes. All come with the child's name knitted in. Write for the brochure and yarn samples:
Knitwits, Route 30, Bondville, VT 05340 (Blanket and bonnet, $30.00; toddler bonnet with pompom, $11.00; hooded sweatshirt, $20.00)

Oshkosh B'Gosh Play-O-Alls
Tough, sanforized denim overalls with hickory stripes. Just like grown-ups wear — pockets, hardware, and all. Sizes 1–6 and 8. Ask for a free catalogue.
Miles Kimball, 35 Algoma Blvd., Oshkosh, WI 54901 (Approx. $12.00)

that you hold her gently by the shoulders and rotate her in a circular motion to the side and up, so that Baby will not have to go through exaggerated and uncomfortable adjustments in order to support her heavy head.

Dressing a baby is done most securely when the baby is lying face down across your lap. You put her hands into her shirt one at a time, and then gently roll her over on your arm toward yourself to finish dressing. As Baby gets older and can sit up, it's best to dress her sitting on the floor. Sit baby between your legs, with her back resting against you while you slip her clothes on. Toddlers are much easier to control this way, too.

DRESSING EQUIPMENT

Birch Dressing Table

The simple lines of this sturdy table make upkeep easy. The raised sides help keep Baby safe, while shelves conveniently hold diapers and clothes close at hand. Pad and safety belt are included. From the Skandia Birch Group manufactured by:

Hedstrom Co., Bedford, PA 15522 (Approx. $89.00)

HOW TO DRESS A BABY

From their extensive work with babies, Dr. Hans Dobler, a German physician, and his associates have formulated some simple suggestions for handling a baby. Their methods help Baby to feel more secure through a great deal of physical contact with her mother.

First, Dr. Dobler suggests that it's better to pick up Baby face down; this way, Baby's instinctive fear of falling backward and her uncomfortable attempts to support her head are avoided. This approach also strengthens the neck muscles that she will soon be using to raise her head.

To pick up a baby when she's on her back, first grasp her under her arms. With one hand gently roll her over onto your other arm so that she's face down. One arm is now under the baby's chest and that hand is holding her opposite arm firmly. Put your other hand between the baby's legs to support her tummy. To put her down, use the same technique in reverse. Place her face down on the mat or dressing table and then, grasping her under her arms, gently roll her over toward you onto your arm to support her back. Then gently slip your arm out from under her.

Dr. Dobler also suggests that you not pull an older baby up from a lying to a sitting position directly, but

Small Changer

A molded plastic changing surface that fits over the side bars of your crib. The Small Changer has a brightly patterned pad and a safety belt. Be sure to use it in the center of the crib so that Baby will land on the padded mattress should she manage to free herself. Manufactured by:
"Strolee" of California, 19067 S. Reyes Ave., Compton, CA 90221 (Approx. $15.00)

A Treasury of Needlecraft Gifts for the New Baby
Jean Ray Laury
Taplinger Publishing Co., 200 Park Ave. South, NYC 10003 ($12.95)
A myriad of projects for parents and friends of babies. The book includes directions for quilted buntings, fabric picture books, bright terry bibs, and dressing gowns.

Note: Not all manufacturers and publishers will accept single orders for a product or book. Always write them first, before sending money, to be certain that they will accept your order and make sure that you have the most recent price, including shipping and handling charges.

LITERATURE OF INTEREST

Beautiful Baby Clothes to Crochet, Knit, Sew and Embroider
Nan Mensinga-Biasiny
Simon & Schuster, 1230 Avenue of the Americas, NYC 10020 ($4.95, paperback)
The prizes of this book are the baby buntings, such as the toasty-warm forest green one with colorful flowers embroidered on it. Other offerings include sweaters, booties, and snowsuits.

"Knit and Crochet Babies' Wardrobe" (Golden Hands Special #19)
Golden Hands, 6 Commercial St., Hicksville, NY 11801 ($2.00)
Directions for making a marvelous striped baby bunting with a hood and zipper front, crib blankets, winter hats and sweaters, and even a knitted toddler's coat. Perfect for needle-happy grandparents!

Sew for Baby the Fun Way
Kerstin Martensson
Kwik-Sew Co., 300 Sixth Ave. N., Minneapolis, MN 55401 ($4.95)
Instructions for sewing a complete wardrobe for Baby's first year. Includes a master pattern for all the garments shown in the book.

Diapers and Toilet Training

Fabric diapers generally come in three types: prefolded, flat, and contoured. The prefolded diapers, shaped to fit any baby, are the best buy. They aren't as absorbent as flat diapers — but neither are they as bulky. Newborn babies use about a hundred diapers a week; so four dozen should be an adequate supply if you do laundry twice a week.

Many mothers have switched completely to disposable diapers, which can be purchased nearly everywhere, including discount drug and department stores. The best way to discard them is to put them in a covered diaper pail lined with a plastic garbage bag; when the pail is full, tie the top of the bag and throw it away. Disposable diapers are not flushable, whatever manufacturers claim. They clog drains and pipes and do not break up as advertised. They are the most expensive answer to diapering. The plastic in disposable diapers is not biodegradable, and putting diapers in garbage pails is a potentially dangerous health hazard. Contact with human waste matter by garbage collectors and flies can spread dangerous diseases such as typhoid fever. Also, some babies are allergic to the plastic part of the diapers. Aside from these drawbacks, disposable diapers are very good for traveling and may be just the answer for a tired new mother.

Another alternative is a diaper service. The diapers you receive from a diaper service are super-clean — in fact, they've been sterilized. A diaper service is less expensive than paper diapers but more expensive than doing-it-yourself. Diaper-service diapers are softer and more comfortable for Baby than paper diapers. Diaper-service babies are less likely to have diaper rash problems than those using home-laundered diapers. The secret lies in the use of very hot water and mild detergents, and many, many rinsings. You ought to consider using a diaper service for the first two months after Baby is born, when you particularly need rest and time to be with him. A month or two of diaper service is a fantastic gift to give expectant parents!

DIAPER CARE

Diapers that sit in a pail for a long time begin to develop a strong-smelling ammonia that is somehow thought to contribute to diaper rash. Here are some suggestions for preventive diaper care:

• Buy a small diaper pail and keep it three-quarters full of water to which a teaspoonful of a Borax solution has been added. (A small pail is best because water-soaked diapers become extremely heavy to tote to the washing machine; and a pail with a locking top will be handy later for keeping your inquisitive tot out.)

• Empty Baby's bowel movements into the toilet and then jiggle the diaper several times while flushing the toilet to be sure that the diaper is rinsed well. Rinse diapers that have only urine on them in the toilet. Wring out the diapers and then put them into the Borax solution.

• Wash diapers in a detergent, using the hottest cycle on the machine. Don't add fabric softener or other chemicals that might irritate a newborn's skin. Never use enzyme presoaks for diapers — even after washing, the chemicals remain and can be absorbed by Baby's skin.

• If your baby shows any signs of redness in the diaper area, begin putting the diapers through a second wash cycle in clear water without soap in order to remove all residues. Dry diapers in the sun, when possible.

DIAPER PINS

Diaper pins are dangerous. They stab and scratch babies and are even swallowed. For this reason, it's important that you close the pins whenever they are not in use — don't carry them in your mouth and don't stick them in anything. Close them as soon as you take them off Baby. A second precaution is always to keep your finger between the pin you're sticking in the diaper and Baby. Your fingers will be scarred, but your baby will be safe.

Don't buy or use diaper pins with plastic heads. These pins — with heads shaped like ducks or other animals — break easily into sharp pieces, leaving an exposed, dangerous metal tip. Metal diaper clips are not recommended because of their small size. They could be swallowed and sucked into the windpipe, causing suffocation.

A NOTE ON TOILET TRAINING

"Toilet training," as one mother I know put it, "is a choice between changing a thousand diapers a day or making a thousand trips to the potty a day." This is particularly the case if you begin toilet training before the baby is truly able to succeed, because of an immature muscular system. Most pediatric specialists suggest that a child should be able to follow simple commands and be able to indicate what he wants clearly before any attempt is made to train him. The longer you wait to begin training, the easier it will be. Around two years of age is a good time for training, because by then your tot will have a drive toward self-reliance and maturity that will work with you to make it easier.

It's helpful to get an idea of when to expect your toddler to wet before trying to work with him on using the pot. You might keep a record for a day or so. Some mothers have found that removing diapers completely helps in getting a child to use the potty because he becomes more conscious of what he's doing and is more likely to control himself. It's as though he had a rule that tells him diapers are for wetting.

Training should be a positive experience and not a punishment process. It's best to have a potty that's just the right size for your tot and sits on the floor. That way, he can use it himself much more easily and will not experience any fear of falling or the discomfort of hanging his legs over the edge of a large, adult-sized toilet. When he graduates to the regular toilet, he may feel more secure straddling the seat while facing the tank.

Toilet Training in Less than a Day, listed at the end of this section, will help you to clarify exactly how to proceed so as to insure success for you and your child. Good luck!

DIAPERS AND ACCESSORIES

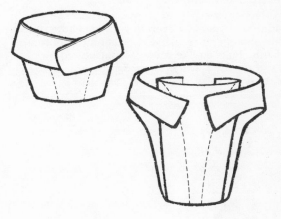

Dexter B-29 Diapers

A patented contour diaper that will fit any baby, from newborn to a three-year-old. A built-in polyurethane foam material soaks up moisture while letting air circulate through the diaper. Double-diapering for nighttime doesn't add to the bulk between the legs as it would with regular diapers. These diapers are very durable, too, and will hold up to many washings. Order from:

Dexter Diaper Factory, P.O. Box 7367, Houston, TX 77008 ($2.00 for a sample diaper; $16.00 a dozen + 10% handling)

Dub-L-Lox Diaper Pins

A rustless, stainless steel diaper pin with a sliding metal safety head that locks the pin closed. They're easy to use and won't open accidentally. Order from:

J. L. Garceau, DeRonde Plastics Corp., 23 Berlin St., P.O. Drawer D, Montpelier, VT 05602 (3 for 35¢)

Sleepy-Drye Outer Pants for Diapers

An all-cotton water-repellent diaper cover that keeps wetness in the diaper and everything outside dry. Great when Baby has a diaper rash and you don't want to use plastic pants. Pulls on like pants. Manufactured by: *Kleinert's, P.O. Box 248, Kutztown, PA 19530 (Approx. $3.00)*

Waterproof Nylon Pants

Very durable pants that withstand machine-washing and drying without becoming brittle. The pull-on style is best because it avoids the sharp-edged seams of snap-on pants. Recommended for babies who develop a rash from contact with plastic. Manufactured by: *Kleinert's, P.O. Box 248, Kutztown, PA 19530 (Approx. $3.00)*

Diaper Dip

A handy plastic clip (#659) for soaking and washing diapers that hooks onto the toilet seat. It saves bending down and prevents losing a diaper when flushing. (You'll still have to wring them out, unfortunately!) Manufactured by: *The Reddy Co., Inc., R.F.D. #2, Montpelier, VT 05602 (Under $2.00)*

Child's Potty

An exquisite design imported from Finland, this sturdy, tip-resistant potty can be emptied from the top — a worksaving feature! The edges are nicely smoothed, including the front shield area. Available in brown or bright red. Order from: *Children's Design Center, 29 Excelsior Springs Ave., Saratoga Springs, NY 12866 ($15.00 + $1.75 postage)*

Saddle Potty

An inexpensive potty with a broad base for stability, this model is ideal for storing in the trunk of the car for emergency use when no service station is in sight. Available in the infant section of stores. Manufactured by:
Glenco Infant Items/Tommee Tippee, 108 Fairway Ct., Northvale, NJ 07647 (Under $5.00)

Zip-Pin

This is a bright, permanently sealed container that holds a solid lubricant for keeping diaper pins slick. Choose yellow, pink, or blue. A pair of matching diaper pins are included in the box. Order from:
The Zip-Pin Co., P.O. Box 28654, Memphis, TN 38128 ($2.50 or 3/$7.00)

Lock-Top Diaper Pail

A unique handle design allows parents to lock the pail lid to keep curious tots out. Other nice features of this pail are its locking deodorizer compartment and the recessed hand holds at the base, which facilitate emptying. Available in yellow or white at retail stores carrying First Years products. Manufactured by:
Kiddie Products, Inc., Avon, MA 02322 (Approx. $6.00)

"Little Guys" Toilet Adapter

A marvelous contraption that sits under the adult toilet ring to make the seat tot-size. There's no need to worry about the adapter coming loose. The deflector that comes with the seat is soft and flexible for safety. The back support can be removed for use by older tots. Manufactured by:
Sybar Corp., 5935 West Irving Park Rd., Chicago, IL 60634 (Approx. $7.00)

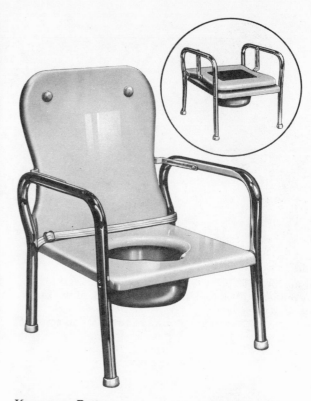

Diaper Duck

A plastic diaper holder for the toilet. Water can be squeezed out of the diaper by pulling the dry end through the Duck. Order from:
F&H Baby Products, Box 2228, Evansville, IN 47714 ($4.49)

Kewaunee Potty

This yellow or white enameled wooden chair has the virtue of being both a potty and a stepstool for a tot. The high chrome sidearms help tots to lower themselves. The pot empties from the back but moves smoothly on railings. In stores, or order from:
Kewaunee Equipment Co., Box 186, Kewaunee, WI 54216 ($18.95 + $1.00 handling)

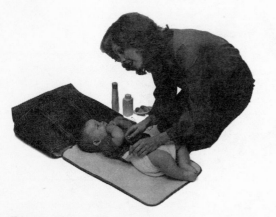

Diaper Changer Bag

The best feature of this diaper bag is its detachable, foam-padded changing pad. The bag has a water repellent cotton canvas exterior with a vinyl detachable inside pocket for soiled diapers. Available with a blue canvas base and your choice of green, red, or linen canvas top. Order from:
It's My Bag, 101 Enfield Place, Syracuse, NY 13214 ($29.95 + $1.50 postage)

Schatzie-Tote

A well-designed pad for diaper-changing at home or on trips. The thick foam padding is covered by leather-look vinyl. A pocket on the side accommodates a diaper or bottle. Straps on the sides and ends can be used to make the foldup pad into either a purse-like diaper bag or a balanced baby carrier. There's a restraining belt in the center for maximum safety. Light blue. Order from:
Swiss Enterprise, Inc., 9840 W. 44th Ave., Wheat Ridge, CO 80033 ($24.50 + $2.00 postage and handling)

Back Pack Bag

A bright yellow nylon water-repellent bag that can be carried by handles or slipped on your back to leave your hands free for Baby. The cotton shoulder straps are adjustable. There's a zippered outside compartment for a bottle and a large inside compartment for diapers and other items. Order from:

Lil' Lovins', P.O. Box 3114, Nashua, NH 03061 ($10.95 + $1.00 postage)

Shoulder Stroller Bag

A snap system allows this all-fabric bag to be converted from a shoulder bag to a stroller or carriage bag. A large pocket compartment in front of the bag holds extra diapers or supplies. The bag comes in red, beige, or navy, in washable quilted cotton fabric. Order from:

Sandbox Industries, 330 Fifth Ave., NYC 10001 ($22.00 + $1.75 postage and handling)

LEAFLETS AND BOOKS ON TOILET TRAINING

No More Diapers

Joae Graham, M.D./Boston Children's Medical Center
Delacorte/Seymour Lawrence, 1 Dag Hammarskjöld Plaza, 245 E. 47th St., NYC 10017 ($3.95, paperback)
An illustrated story book for children about the toilet training of a little boy and a little girl. Includes instructions and suggestions for parents.

"Successful Toilet Training"

T. Berry Brazelton, M.D.
Pamphlet No. 751, Service Editor, Baby Talk Magazine, 66 E. 34th St., NYC 10016 (30¢ + 75¢ service charge)
A helpful leaflet that suggests very clearly how to proceed with toilet training. It also gives statistics suggesting that around two years of age is the most common time to institute training successfully.

Toilet Learning: A Guide for Parent and Child

Alison Mack
Little, Brown & Co., 34 Beacon St., Boston, MA 02114 ($6.95)
A picture book for a child combined with a book for parents about toilet training. Humorous parts of the book show firemen, policemen, and other figures in a small child's life sitting on the toilet. My only objection to the book is its drawings of big pipes carrying "wee-wee" and "doo-doo," which don't help ease a youngster's fear of being flushed away by accident along with the waste. The grownup part of the book is excellent.

Toilet Training in Less than a Day

Nathan H. Azrin and Richard M. Foxx
Pocket Books, 1230 Ave. of the Americas, NYC 10020 ($1.75, paperback)
A very clear guide to an all-out toilet training campaign that demonstrates to a child irrevocably and indisputably exactly what you want him to do from this day forth. Uses a clear-cut reward system and details the exact skills that you want your child to master. Clear illustrations of a child potty-training make this a useful storybook during your campaign.

> **Note:** Not all manufacturers and publishers will accept single orders for a product or book. Always write them first, before sending money, to be certain that they will accept your order and make sure that you have the most recent price, including shipping and handling charges.

Feeding

THE BOTTLE BATTLE

The most important part of a baby's bottle is the nipple. It is essential that the nipple be the right size for Baby and that it provide the right mouth action for her, maximizing the development of her mouth and cheek muscles and insuring proper alignment of her teeth.

One manufacturer claims that its nipple is "so like mother herself" and, to reinforce the idea, pictures a baby nursing at her mother's breast. The rubber nipple has been made to look just like its human counterpart. This advertising is misleading, because studies have shown that nursing from the breast and sucking at a rubber nipple are two entirely different actions.

During breastfeeding, the mother's nipple and the areola, the entire colored area surrounding the nipple, are taken into Baby's mouth; the nipple stretches beyond Baby's gums up to the roof of her mouth. She relies on the friction created by pulling the nipple back into the top of her mouth and pushing on it with her tongue from underneath to get milk. All the muscles of her lips, cheeks, tongue, and jaws are brought into play. And it's hard work! Some babies even have beads of perspiration dripping down their foreheads and blush a bright rosy red from the effort required.

In contrast, when a rubber nipple is used, the milk flows directly into Baby's throat with barely any effort on her part. She pushes her tongue forward, rather than backward. Her lips are pursed outward rather than tightened downward. Her cheek muscles are relaxed. She presses the rubber nipple against her upper gums with her tongue to stop the flow of milk long enough to swallow. This abnormal tongue thrusting and swallowing pattern may lead to lisping and incorrect use of the tongue in talking. It may also cause a space to develop between the front teeth later, affecting bite.

Some researchers feel that babies have very strong sucking needs, which are met by long sucking sessions at the breast but are not met adequately in the time that it takes to drain a bottle. They postulate that later thumb, finger, and pacifier sucking are the young child's way of making up for its unmet sucking needs.

In selecting a rubber nipple, it's important that the milk not come out of it too easily and that the nipple be the right size for your baby, not going too far back in her mouth, but resting comfortably against the roof of her mouth. You need to allow time for Baby to suck and exercise her mouth beyond the drinking process. A well-designed pacifier may answer this need when she is very young.

Warning: *Never tie the pacifier around your baby's neck!* Babies have died from strangulation when pacifier cords became entangled in their cribs.

BOTTLE-FEEDING TECHNIQUES

The best approach to giving your baby her bottle is to take her in your arms and hold her closely while she drinks. Feeding time is the most joyous time in a baby's life, and it's important that you be on hand to share it with her. Talk gently to her while looking at her eye to eye. Try to relax and enjoy this time together. Some authorities suggest that you alternate letting her lie on the left or the right side so that both eyes can get practice focusing on you.

If you have to let Baby feed herself occasionally, *be sure to prop her into a semi-upright position* on a firm cushion and in a safe place, preferably on the floor, where she won't be in danger of falling. There is mounting evidence that babies who are allowed to lie on their backs while sucking milk from a bottle are more likely to develop inner-ear infections. It's thought to be caused by milk being forced into the inner canals of the ear when swallowing horizontally. Unfortunately, a straight-neck bottle forces Baby into a headback position even when she is being held for feeding. (The numerous bottle proppers on the market are not recommended because most of them still force Baby into a drinking position on her back. They also encourage mothers to leave Baby to herself when she should be held and talked to.)

Another good bottle-feeding practice is not to let Baby take the bottle to bed with her for naps and at night. "Baby-bottle tooth decay" can result; this is caused by Baby falling asleep while sucking. Milk or juice remains pooled around the teeth, setting up a perfect environment for tooth decay. These cavities — most frequently found in older babies and tots — may also lead to inflamed gums and immature speech patterns.

BOTTLES AND PACIFIERS

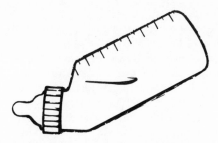

Corecto Feeding Bottle
An angle-necked plastic bottle that places the nipple in a horizontal position so that Baby's head is semi-upright while nursing. Because of the angle of the bottle, liquids flow into the nipple and air swallowing becomes less of a problem. Combine the Corecto Bottle with a Nuk Nipple for an ideal match. To order, write: *Royal Products, Inc., P.O. Box 90312, East Point, GA 30344 (8/$5.16 + $2.00 postage and handling)*

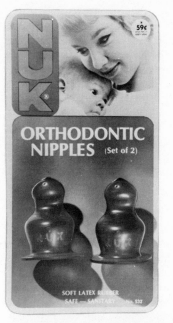

Nuk Nipple and Orthodontic Exerciser
The Nuk Nursing Nipple (#532) conforms to the shape of Baby's palate, collapsing and expanding naturally. The flat passage encourages closed lips and nasal breathing. The nipple fits all standard bottles. An over-the-bottle "Playtex-style" nipple is also available. The Exerciser (#530) is identical to the nipple, except that it has a firm plastic shield. To find the store nearest you, write:
Reliance Products Corp., 108 Mason St., Woonsocket, RI 02895 (Nipple, 2/$1.30; Exerciser, $1.00; "Playtex-style," $2.00)

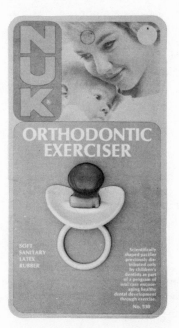

BEGINNING SOLIDS

What age to begin solids? This is a question that's on most mothers' minds as Baby leaves the newborn stage. Sometimes mothers compete with each other this way, bragging about how early little Duncan began solids and how much he eats. Actually, there should be no rush to begin solids. There's no medical proof that "the earlier the better." In fact, the American Academy of Pediatrics has stated that formula or breastmilk provides all the nutrients your baby needs until she's six months old.

Your baby must learn how to chew and swallow foods; it's not automatic, regardless of how old she is when you begin. Soft foods like cream of rice or mashed banana are good for openers, but ask your pediatrician for recommendations. It takes time to learn to handle pieces of food — some babies swallow chunks that are too large, only to gag them back up. Choking in babies who are learning to eat happens frequently and is seldom serious. Simply stay close and talk gently to your baby until things are back to normal. The time to become concerned is when she changes color and seems to have difficulty breathing. If this happens, hold her upside-down, or face-down on your lap with her head hanging over your knees; then give her a sharp pat between her shoulder blades to dislodge the piece. Caution: Raw honey has been implicated in a serious form of infant botulism that can be fatal. Parents are warned not to feed honey to babies under one year of age.

Commercially prepared baby foods and juices are not recommended for the following reasons:
• The major ingredient that you are purchasing in most baby foods is water! They also contain unneeded sugar, starches, and other additives.
• They are packaged in clear jars, causing the loss of light-sensitive vitamins in vegetables.
• They are unduly expensive, compared to home-prepared vegetables and meats.

FIXING YOUR OWN BABY FOOD

Two products that you may want to consider buying, which will pay you back in years of service, are an electric blender and a pressure cooker. You don't need a fancy blender with numerous buttons — a few speeds will do. The Osterizer Blender (made by the Oster Manufacturing Co.) has an optional Mini-Blend Jar that allows you to process a cup or less of baby food and then store it in the same jar. A pressure cooker is a good investment because it is easy to use, retains much of the food's natural vitamins, and cooks very quickly. Sliced carrots or vanilla custard can be cooked in three minutes and potatoes in ten. A pressure cooker is good, too, for making beef stew (in less than an hour), which can be blended for the new eater or served as finger food for the old pro. (See the end of this chapter for a listing of good baby-food cookbooks.)

FINGER FOODS

Toward the end of the first year, Baby will enjoy feeding herself small tidbits. It will help her to develop finger and hand coordination, too. Here are some suggestions for finger foods:
Cheerios
Small cheese chunks or strips
Pieces of mushy fruits such as banana, cantaloupe, and tomato
Canned sweet peas
Avocado chunks
Chunks of well-cooked, unstringy vegetables such as potatoes, carrots, and sweet potatoes
Small pieces of hard-boiled egg
(Avoid peanuts, corn, and popcorn, as they can cause choking and even suffocation or pneumonia when lodged in the windpipe.)

FEEDING AIDS

Although this chapter lists many spoons and dishes, there are only a few features worth looking for when purchasing eating utensils and plates for a new self-feeder. The spoon, at best, should have a shallow bowl that can be easily emptied by a baby. The dish should be unbreakable and feature sharply angled, high sides so that Baby can scrape food onto her spoon. A heavy dish or some way of fastening the dish to the table such as a lump of clay or a suction pad is a must. Many mothers have enjoyed using training cups that have a weighted base, a nonspill top, and two easy-to-grip handles for the intermediate stage between bottle and glass. Baby still delights in turning these cups upside-down to watch milk dribble out, but at least you can catch her before the milk's all gone.

Toddler mealtime is not for the orderly or weak-stomached. Food goes everywhere — in Baby's hair, on the floor, in her cup. It's better to approach it all with restraint and call it a learning experience than to get uptight about it. Buy a good, big strip of heavy plastic or oilcloth to go under her chair and then sit back and try to let things go. It's probably less messy to take the plate away as soon as she begins to dawdle, and, rather than keeping her cup on her table, to offer it after the meal or when she asks for it.

Baby Bottle Straw

The Sit-N-Sip Baby Bottle Straw can be placed in any standard-sized baby bottle. It allows Baby to sit up and drink. Good for infants in the last stages of bottle sucking. For "where to find it" information, write: *MEDI, Inc., 27 Maple Ave., P.O. Box 325, Holbrook, MA 02343 (Under $1.00)*

Washable Food Catcher

Better than the standard flat bib, the Kangaroo Bib is made of flexible colored plastic and features a "pouch" for catching dropped food and liquids. Wash it in warm soapsuds after each meal. Presto! It's ready to be used again. A must for beginning eaters and toddlers! Available at J. C. Penney stores. Manufactured by: *Glenco Infant Items, Inc./Tommee Tippee, 108 Fairway Ct., Northvale, NJ 07647 (Approx. $1.25)*

Cup and Flatware

A fine collection of eating aids in hand-polished steel. The cup has a wide handle for easy grasping. The spoons are carefully balanced to aid the beginning eater. The steel is resistant to food chemicals, does not add a metallic taste to foods, and is unaffected by detergents or dishwashing. Write for a free catalogue, and order from: *Fraser's WMF Stainless, Division of WMF of America, Inc., 85 Price Pkwy., Farmingdale, NY 11735 (Baby feeding spoon, $7.50; child's cup, $8.50; baby spoon and fork set, $14.50)*

Spillable Cloth

The Spillable Cloth is a 45" heavy-duty vinyl mat that serves as a catch-all when placed under Baby's high-chair. It's silk-screened with a large orange duck that says "I'll Catch your Quackers." Order from: *Barbistuff, 635 Tuallitan Rd., Los Angeles, CA 90049 ($6.98 + $1.00 postage and handling)*

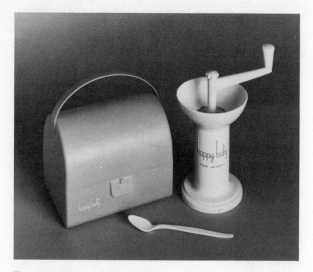

Food Grinder for the Table

Now you can make baby food right at the table, even in restaurants! The Happy Baby Food Grinder processes cooked meats, fruits, and vegetables with a few turns of the handle. The baby food appears at the top, ready to be spooned into Baby's mouth. It has a stainless steel cutting blade and may be taken apart for washing or sterilizing. Model #800 comes with a spoon and carrying case. The texture of the food can be varied by adding more or less liquid. Order from:
Bowland-Jacobs International, Inc., Fox Industrial Park, Yorkville, IL 60560 ($8.50 + $1.00 shipping and handling)

Baby Food Jar Lifter

No more burned fingers! Use this screw-on cap in place of the regular cap, heat jar in water, and then lift out. Lifter has twenty ridges that grip the jar firmly, plus a hinged top for feeding that snaps shut for storage. Can be sterilized. Order from:
Gift Fair, P.O. Box 115, Riverside, CT 06878 ($1.25 + 75¢ postage)

Sta-Put Feeding Dish

A sturdy plastic vise fastens this feeding dish directly to Baby's highchair or feeding table so that she can't overturn it. The dish itself has three easy-to-see compartments that are steep enough to help her push food onto her spoon. Dishwasher-safe and unbreakable. The vise can be removed for the older toddler.
Kelron Industries, Inc., 350 Sharon Park Dr., Suite J-1, Menlo Park, CA 94025 ($6.95)

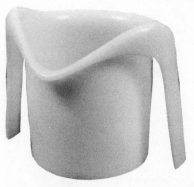

Training Cup

The curved lip and easy-grip side handles of this cup make it ideal for beginning self-feeders. Break-resistant plastic. Available in drug and variety stores carrying Reliance baby products. Manufactured by:
Reliance Products Corp., 108 Mason St., Woonsocket, RI 02895 (Under $1.00)

Night n' Day Medicine Spoon

This lighted, indexed spoon makes it simple to measure out a dose and keep it level from bottle to mouth. The glow of the spoon fascinates tots and makes it a bit easier to persuade them to take medications. Order from:
Gus File, Inc., P.O. Box 3006, Albuquerque, NM 87110 ($3.00 postpaid)

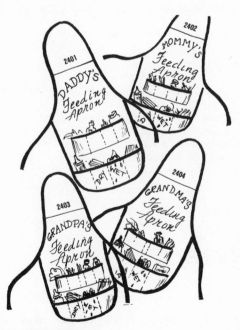

Feeding Aprons

Choose from: "Daddy's Apron" (#2401), "Mommy's Apron" (#2402), "Grandpa's Apron" (#2403), and "Grandma's Apron" (#2404). Each is screen-printed cotton with front pockets. Machine washable. Order from:
Mary Jane Co., 4033 Sunset Blvd., Hollywood, CA 90020 ($5.00)

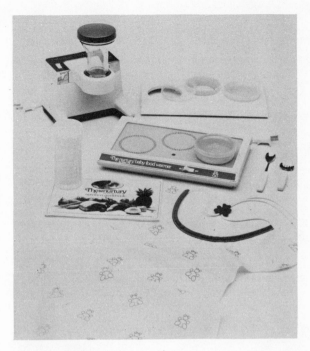

Feeding Helpers

You don't need to invest in the whole Nurtury Feeding System to take advantage of its nicely designed accessories. The Feeding Helpers (Model A-1) include a feeding spoon, a baby's self-feeding spoon, a dishwasher-safe training tumbler, a large machine-washable bib, three dishwasher-safe food servers with lids, and a nutrition guidebook. (The electric baby-food grinder and food warmer are sold separately.) Order from:
Teledyne Water Pik, 1730 East Prospect St., Fort Collins, CO 80521 ($14.95 + $1.00 postage and handling)

Cereal Bowl

A steep-sided bright yellow plastic bowl with a suction base, which has a tab for easy removal from tray or table. Write for a catalogue of baby products.
Mothercare-by-Mail, 196 Quaker Bridge Mall, U.S. Rt. 1 and Quaker Bridge Rd., Lawrenceville, NJ 08648 (Approx. $3.50)

Scooper Bowl and Scooper Plate

The deep slopes of these bright dishes encourage Baby to spoon-feed herself. Both bowls are dishwasher-safe when the rubber bottom rims are removed. Available in the infant department of stores. Manufactured by: *Glenco Infant Items, Inc./Tommee Tippee, 108 Fairway Ct., Northvale, NJ 07647 (Each under $5.00)*

PUBLICATIONS OF INTEREST

Baby Feasts from Family Meals and **Osterizer Guide for Feeding Baby Better**
Oster Corp., 5055 N. Lydell Ave., Milwaukee, WI 53217 (Free; and 50¢)
Simple recipe ideas and how-to suggestions for making baby food.

The Complete Guide to Preparing Baby Foods at Home
Sue Castle
Doubleday & Company, Inc., 501 Franklin St., Garden City, NY 11530 ($6.95)
An excellent source book for do-it-yourself baby-food cookery. Contains a thorough discussion of nutrition, equipment suggestions, good recipes, and an appendix giving the nutritional value of foods.

Feeding Your Baby During His First Year
Food Before Six: A Feeding Guide for Parents of Young Children
Order from your local Dairy Council or write: National Dairy Council, 111 N. Canal St., Chicago, IL 60606 (Free)
Two very practical leaflets with excellent suggestions regarding meal planning for little ones.

Feed Me, I'm Yours
Vicki Lansky
Meadowbrook Press, 16648 Meadowbrook Ln., Wayzata, MN 55391 ($3.50)
A spiral-bound cookbook that includes suggestions for nutritious baby foods, finger foods, snacks, breakfast ideas; it also contains marvelous suggestions by age for birthday parties. (A mass-market paperback edition is available for $2.25, from Bantam Books.)

Instant Baby Food
Linda McDonald
Oaklawn Press, 283 South Lake Ave., Suite 200, Pasadena, CA 91101 ($3.95, paperback)
Tells how to use a baby-food grinder to prepare meals for your baby. Gives suggestions about nutrition and ideas for milk drinks, and tells how to prepare basic foods as well as quick variations.

Making Your Own Baby Food
Mary Turner and James Turner
Bantam Books, Inc., 666 Fifth Ave., NYC 10019 ($1.75, paperback)
Not just a recipe book — a consumer's statement about the dangers of processed baby food and the increasingly poor nutrition of Americans. Includes reading suggestions and product sources.

The Natural Baby Food Cookbook
Margaret Kenda and Phyllis Williams
Avon Books, 959 Eighth Ave., NYC 10019 ($1.50, paperback)
A jewel of a book! It contains an easy-to-follow schedule of what to introduce when, lists nutrients and what foods have them, and has a helpful chapter called "The Finicky, Fussy, Sick or Busy Child." Provides recipes for making your own yoghurt, teething biscuits, and cottage cheese, if you're so inclined.

No-Nonsense Nutrition for Your Baby's First Year
Jo-Ann Heslin, Annette B. Natow, and Barbara C. Raven
CBI Publishing Co., Boston, MA 02210 ($6.95)
A superb handbook for answering your questions about feeding Baby. Part of the book is in a question-and-answer format. There are also recipes, suggestions for diet while traveling, vegetarian diet ideas, ideas for dealing with problem feeding times, suggestions for food preparation, and a list of drugs excreted in human milk. The most up-to-date baby nutrition handbook available!

Proctor-Silex Blended Baby Food
Miriam Sursa, Consumer Relations, Proctor-Silex, Inc., 700 W. Tabor Rd., Philadelphia, PA 19120 (Free)
Six recipes, including carrot custard and babies' chicken soup.

Note: Not all manufacturers and publishers will accept single orders for a product or book. Always write them first, before sending money, to be certain that they will accept your order and make sure that you have the most recent price, including shipping and handling charges.

Nursery Decoration

It's current nursery philosophy to put Baby on stilts for his parents' convenience. The crib, the dressing table — every piece of furniture is up on legs. It's all designed for standing adults and not really for babies. Putting a twisting, turning, squirming little tot up high is inviting disaster. One out of every two babies falls from a high surface at least once before one year of age, and one study has estimated that each year over 100,000 infants require hospitalization because of falls!

Contributing to our "stilted" approach to furniture is the feeling we have that floors are dirty, drafty, or somehow unfit for babies. So babies are confined to playpens, cribs, dressing tables, walkers, jumpers, and a number of other inventions rather than given "floor freedom." Studies by psychologists have found "floor" babies to score higher on intelligence tests than babies who have led restricted lives.

A safer, more enjoyable approach for your baby is for your family to become floor-oriented. More and more parents are getting down to baby level. Why not change Baby's diapers on a pad on the floor? You'll eliminate the danger of falls, Plus, your independent toddler will be less insulted than when he's removed from play and held up on tables for changes.

Let's start planning the nursery from the floor up. Leaving a smooth area for rolling toys and floor play later, carpet the area under the crib and dressing table (if you want to use one) for protective cushioning. One couple I know installed play steps in one corner of their children's room. The steps were constructed of plywood nailed onto frames and covered with a thick carpeting. The steps could be used as seats or for climbing and jumping.

Or you might like to make a large, cushiony play pad by covering a single mattress in a washable fabric and surrounding it on all sides by a giant doughnut of a bolster made out of muslin stuffed with shredded foam and covered in the same fabric as the mattress.

Look at the wall from a tot's viewpoint and think about crayon-proofing it by using washable paint or brightly patterned vinyl-coated wallpaper. If you don't want to wallpaper a whole wall, consider putting up an easy wallpaper border just at baby level. Your local paint store probably has a number of bright patterns. Place an unbreakable mirror at a crawler's eye level so that he can see himself.

Away with bland pastels! Babies love colors and patterns. One study found that babies choose bright yellows and reds over all other colors, and pictures of human faces over all other designs. They also showed a preference for bold geometric patterns. Bring these patterns down to baby level with posters.

You'll want diapers and clothes easily within reach with one hand — you're bound to have a baby in the other. Think about open shelving using plastic bins rather than awkward, two-handed drawers. The same shelves can later be used to hold toys. If you have a carpenter in the family, consider making shelving units out of brightly painted wooden boxes that have smoothly rounded edges. They could later provide hours of play for a toddler who loves climbing in, out, and over things.

Window shades are a necessity! Babies are like roosters — they rise at the crack of dawn unless a good shade can convince them that it's still dark outside. Blinds are a poorer choice for several reasons: they are more difficult to keep clean; they don't eliminate light as well as shades do; and toddlers have accidentally been strangled in the cords.

Many parents have found that an aquarium is a good

way of providing a night light, a gentle sound for soothing Baby to sleep, and a humidifier all in one. Choose big goldfish if you want Baby to see the action.

The best investment that you can make for yourself is a well-padded rocker with arms and a footstool. If you can afford it, buy a swivel platform rocker you can use later in the living room or den. It will give you hundreds of hours of enjoyment during late-night feeding and whenever you want to cuddle and soothe your baby. A good, old-fashioned rocker will do, although it's not as safe; the sharp-edged rockers pose a hazard for a baby who's pulling up or newly walking. A hassock with built-in swivel wheels can be used now by you and later pushed by your toddler as a safe walker. (You may want to remove the wheels so that it will stay in place as you rock.)

Another good investment is a clock with a lighted dial so that you can keep up with the time during the night. (Although you might feel better off not knowing that you're up at 3 A.M.!)

If you're on a tight budget, you can save money by using a sturdy drawer for baby when he's very young and then purchasing a crib that can later be made into a youth bed. For economy, buy shelving rather than a chest, and plan to change Baby on the floor wherever you happen to be, rather than investing in an expensive changing table. Used baby furniture is an excellent buy, so keep an eye on the "for sale" ads. If you decide to repaint furniture, be sure the label states that the paint is nontoxic. Be particularly careful when buying an old crib (see pp. 18–20).

It's really fun to plan a place for Baby! But always keep in mind that your baby won't care about his surroundings as much as he loves being held and talked to by you. It's the people in his life that count the most.

Nursery Wallpaper

The "Who Me?" pattern shows snakes, monkeys, birds, and butterflies hiding in a brilliant jungle of greens, reds, blues, and yellows — a perfect pattern for a very young child! This prepasted wall covering is washable, and a matching fabric is available. This pattern by United DeSoto, and many other patterns like it, are available in hardware and paint stores. Many can be easily stripped off if you want to change patterns or if you live in an apartment. The secret of removal lies in proper wall preparation.

Mite-Hite Light Switch Extension

A small screwdriver plus a few seconds' time are all that's needed to attach the Mite-Hite to a wall switch plate. Your child pulls the rod down to turn the light off, and pushes up to turn it on. A good idea for the bathroom, too! For information or to order, write: *Stephen Shanan Co., Inc., 10107 Westview #211, Houston, TX 77043 ($2.95)*

Wall Mirror

A shatterproof, lightweight mirror made of polyester film backed by polyurethane foam. The reflected image is clear and distortion-free — perfect for toddler self-viewing! You can also use it vertically. Hangs by means of self-adhering pads. Free catalogue available, or order from:
Childcraft Education Corp., 20 Kilmer Rd., Edison, NJ 08817 ($27.95 + shipping and handling)

> **Note:** Not all manufacturers and publishers will accept single orders for a product or book. Always write them first, before sending money, to be certain that they will accept your order and make sure that you have the most recent price, including shipping and handling charges.

Embroidered Birth Sampler Kits

Choose an early American birth announcement with birds and cherubim (No. 6913) or a more modern stork (No. 7450). Each kit contains all you need for lettering and stitching. Available at yarn shops and needlework departments. Manufactured by:
Columbia-Minerva Corp., 295 Fifth Ave., NYC 10016 (Early American, $4.00; Stork, $6.00)

A POORLY DESIGNED PLAYPEN

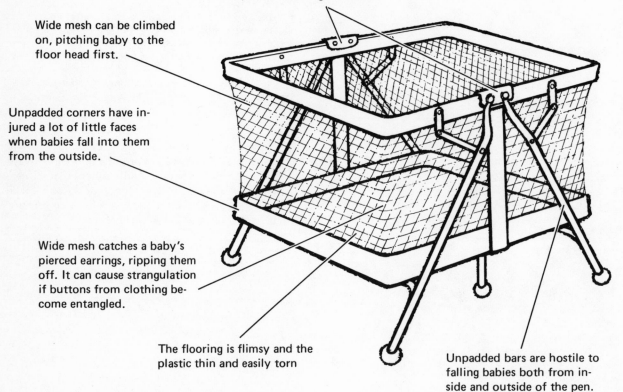

Unguarded hinges have amputated babies' fingers when a parent is raising the side.

Wide mesh can be climbed on, pitching baby to the floor head first.

Unpadded corners have injured a lot of little faces when babies fall into them from the outside.

Wide mesh catches a baby's pierced earrings, ripping them off. It can cause strangulation if buttons from clothing become entangled.

The flooring is flimsy and the plastic thin and easily torn

Unpadded bars are hostile to falling babies both from inside and outside of the pen.

Playpens

In the 1940s and 1950s many mothers felt that playpens were indispensable. In fact, it was a sign of a "spoiled" baby if she couldn't stay contentedly in her pen. Recent studies dispute the value of the playpen — in fact, there is some documentation that babies kept in playpens for long periods of time each day show slower development than babies who are given the freedom to explore from the floor.

Most active, bright crawling babies have a playpen tolerance of about five minutes at a time. And no wonder! Babies need to move and explore. They long to touch things, pull up and move about, and they naturally want to be near their mothers when household chores are underway. More and more young mothers are baby-proofing their homes and then setting their babies free under close supervision. The indispensable playpen ends up in the corner of the living room filled with all of Baby's toys.

Before routinely purchasing a playpen, consider the following facts:

• A safe playpen is an expensive investment for such short use.

• Playpens take up a great deal of floor space, which is an important consideration for apartment and small-home dwellers.

• There are two hazards involved with older mesh playpens that you should know about. Babies have had their fingers amputated by the sharp metal hinges at the top of the pen when a parent was raising the sides, and several babies have been strangled by catching the buttons of their clothing in the mesh.

The advantages of a playpen:

• It may free you temporarily for minor chores. You'll have the security of knowing where Baby is and that she is relatively safe.

• You can put your pen in the trunk of the car and carry it with you when you travel. It can be used as a bed at Grandma's and as a restraining device at the beach or pool, where it would be unsafe for Baby to roam.

The old-fashioned wooden playpen, although it is heavier, has a few advantages over the mesh pen. Wooden pens tend to be sturdier and to have better, more durable flooring than the mesh models. The slatted sides allow a better view of the world and give babies a hold for pulling up to a standing position. While the dangers of hinges and mesh accidents are removed, the chances of head bruises from hitting the slats are increased. Look for a good used model for a bargain, but check to see that it hasn't been painted with paint containing lead and that the slats are close together so that Baby can't get his body through the gaps while entrapping his head.

The Juvenile Products Manufacturers Association, in cooperation with the American Society for Testing and Materials, has recently enacted a voluntary safety standard for mesh and wooden playpens. Playpens that meet this standard are marked with a stamp of approval.

A Summary of the JPMA Playpen Standard

- *The playpen should have no sharp edges, protrusions, or points.* Babies can be hurt by falling onto hardware such as bolt heads in the flooring.
- *The playpen should have no scissoring, cutting, or pinching potential at the hinges.* Babies may sever their fingers when the side of the pen is raised.
- *The playpen should be at least 20 inches high, from the top of the pad to the top of the railing.* Babies sometimes try to climb out of lower pens and get hurt by falling.
- *The floor of the playpen should be able to withstand 80 pounds of static weight and 50 pounds of bouncing weight without giving way.* Babies and tots can cause flimsy flooring to break.
- *Playpen railings should be able to support 50 pounds without breaking or bending, and they should be equipped with a locking device to ensure that the railing does not collapse accidentally and cannot be lowered by a child from outside or inside the pen.* Sides may bend or snap under the weight of heavier babies and may be lowered by children.
- *The bars on wood playpens should be smooth, to avoid splintering. The bars should be no more than 2 3/8 inches apart, so that the baby's body will not slip through the opening while leaving the head behind.* This regulation is intended to prevent strangulation.
- *Openings in the mesh should not be wide enough to entrap a baby's fingers or toes or to ensnare the buttons on baby clothing.* Babies can get hung by entrapped neck buttons on fastened clothing.
- *The following warnings to parents must appear:*
  — The playpen, including side rails, should be fully erect prior to use.
  — Do not add padding or other objects inside the playpen that will permit your child to climb out.
  — The playpen is intended for use by a child who is unable to climb out of it and who weighs less than 30 pounds and is less than 34 inches tall.

Even though many playpens are constructed according to this voluntary standard, another problem has arisen. The vinyl upholstery on many mesh playpens is hazardous for babies who bite into it and get pieces lodged in their throats. A good test for vinyl on playpens and other pieces of baby equipment, such as highchairs, is to pinch the upholstery between your thumb and finger. If it pinches easily and seems thin and flimsy, it may tear later.

Wooden Playpen

A sturdy, well-designed folding playpen with rounded bars for added protection when Baby falls. All sides have teething rails. The pen has a natural birch finish and measures 36" × 36". Comes without a pad. Manufactured by:
Hedstrom Co., Bedford, PA 15522 ($39.00)

Note: Not all manufacturers and publishers will accept single orders for a product or book. Always write them first, before sending money, to be certain that they will accept your order and make sure that you have the most recent price, including shipping and handling charges.

Safety and Poison Prevention

Accidents are the leading cause of death in children. In the U.S. in an average year, 4300 babies and children under five are killed, and for each one killed, four are permanently crippled. One child out of every three sustains an injury requiring medical help. All of us have an "it can't happen to me" attitude about accidents, but they do happen, to children that are just as precious and loved as our own.

As few as fifty baby aspirins, or twelve adult aspirins, can kill a child. Six iron tablets, like the kind pregnant mothers take, can kill a child. It has been reported that 100,000 children are poisoned by aspirin every year and 144 die. Federal regulations have recently gone into effect requiring baby aspirin to be sold only in small amounts and aspirin bottles to have tamper-proof safety caps.

Another four hundred thousand children a year swallow poisonous household products. The Children's Hospital Medical Center in Boston lists the most common poisoners of children:

HOUSEHOLD ITEMS — ammonia, bleach, drain cleaner, oven cleaner, toilet bowl cleaner, corn and wart remover, furniture polish, metal cleaner, typewriter cleaner, gun cleaner, grease remover, carbolic acid disinfectants, strychnine rat poison, strong acids, antifreeze, camphor, arsenic rat poison, DDT insect poison, denatured alcohol, hydrogen peroxide, ink, after-shave lotion, permanent wave solution, nail polish, hair dye, perfume, liquor or beer, washing soda, turpentine, paint thinner, kerosene, gasoline, lighter fluid, wood preservatives, brush cleaner.

MEDICINES — aspirin, "pep" drugs, iron pills and syrup, reducing medicine, some douche preparations, sleep-inducing drugs, laxatives, iodine, eye medicine, heart medicine, tranquilizers, vitamins, paregoric.

A special warning about two poisons:

Lead paint is often eaten by babies and toddlers because they mistake it for candy. They ingest it by chewing on windowsills, crib railings, or other painted surfaces. Putting orange juice or tomato juice in a poorly fired ceramic pitcher with a lead-containing glaze may leach the lead into the juice and cause poisoning. Lead poisoning is slow and must be treated before symptoms even appear. Ask your doctor or local hospital for information about obtaining lead-poisoning tests.

Boric acid is not valuable for diaper rash or any common ailment. Poisoning often occurs when it is mistaken for a baby's formula mix or is used to treat diaper rash. Do not keep boric acid in the house.

TAKE A SAFETY TOUR

As soon as your baby begins to sit up, it's time to take a tour of your home to clear away the hazards that might later cost him his life. Go from room to room.

• *The kitchen.* Let's begin with the stove. Remember, from now on, always turn pot handles to the back of the stove, away from the reach of your curious tot, who might try to pull the pot down to see what's in it. If you have a gas stove, consider removing the knobs when not in use, as soon as your baby gets tall enough to reach them.

Look under the kitchen sink: take all of the strong and very dangerous chemicals out and put them on a high shelf, preferably locked away. Be careful about your dishwasher's cup — babies have scooped out the detergent before anyone could stop them, causing severe mouth burns and even death.

Remove the handles on lower kitchen drawers and put sharp scissors and knives out of reach.

Begin now to unplug electrical appliances and to wrap their cords up so that they won't hang down when in use.

Plan, too, to arrange your day so that you don't have to spend the harrassing 4:00 to 6:00 P.M. time racing madly about the kitchen trying to fix supper with a crying baby underfoot. Make a list of meals, like meatloaf or stew, that you can fix in the morning and put in the oven with little fuss during this peak time of tiredness and stress.

● *The bathroom.* The medicine cabinet is not a safe place to keep medicines. It won't be long until your little one surprises you with his climbing skills. Keep only your harmless needs in the medicine chest, low cabinets, and drawers. Put drugs on the highest shelf of the refrigerator door or under lock and key.

Buy a one-ounce bottle of Ipecac syrup at a drugstore to induce vomiting for poisoning when instructed to do so by your doctor.

Be particularly careful about effervescent denture tablets, which have caused severe mouth burns in babies.

Put razor blades back in the pack — never directly into the trash can.

● *The rest of the house.* The most dangerous item for babies and children in your house is the table! Each year, an estimated 87,000 babies and young children must have emergency room treatment as a result of running into one. Store your living room coffee table away from Baby as a first preventative measure.

Electrical hazards are also a danger to Baby. Look for open electrical outlets. Babies burn their hands by putting bobby pins and other small metal items in the holes. Install safety outlet covers, which are usually available at hardware stores.

All extension cords that aren't absolutely necessary should be removed. Babies receive disfiguring mouth burns when they try to unplug them by holding the cord's head in their mouths. Their saliva forms an electrical arc, and if they are sitting on metal, such as a heating vent, with a wet diaper, they may be electrocuted in seconds. Electrical tape should be wrapped completely around the cord head and the plug that's in it.

Cigarette lighters, matches, glass and decorative objects on low surfaces should be removed. Guns and ammunition should be put under lock and key, broken toys thrown away, and all windows and screens secured against falls.

● *The garage.* Check for poisons such as antifreeze and insecticides. Hammers, saws, lawn mowers, and other sharp implements and tools should be stored in a safe place away from your inquisitive tot.

● *Water holes.* Fill in the lily pond with dirt until the children are older. Check to see that swimming pools are safely protected from wandering babies with a secure fence and a locking gate.

How much better it is to be prepared now than to risk a lifetime of remorse because of carelessness in protecting your toddler! In the long run there is no safety precaution on earth that can replace the constant vigilance of a caring adult — and that's your responsibility! It's tiring and sometimes harassing, but truly a way of loving your child.

THE U.S. CONSUMER PRODUCT SAFETY COMMISSION

The U.S. Consumer Product Safety Commission was activated on May 14, 1973, with the responsibility for protecting the public from unreasonable risks of injury associated with products. The Commission has already acted to make cribs safer, to put child-resistant closures on drugs, and to ban unsafe toys. If your baby has been injured by a product, you can call the U.S. Consumer Product Safety Commission toll free anytime, from anywhere in the continental U.S. The number is: 800-638-8326. In Maryland call: 800-492-8363. For the Virgin Islands, Alaska, Hawaii, and Puerto Rico call: 800-638-8333. A form for reporting hazardous products to the commission has been reproduced for your use at the end of the book.

WAYS OF PROTECTING BABIES

Dr. Clinton B. Lillbridge (in *Clinical Pediatrics,* July 1973) reports an effective system for protecting tots that he designed and tested in his own home. He suggests placing two self-engaging latches or an extra doorknob to close off dangerous stairways and cupboards in which you wish to store poisons or other hazardous items. The value of the two latches or knobs is that they are placed far enough apart so that a toddler cannot simultaneously operate both of them. The system costs less than $2.00 per door and can be purchased at a hardware store.

His specific instructions are as follows:

1. Choose a large cupboard or closet in which to put harmful chemicals. Also, plan to install the system on dangerous stairway doors.

2. Purchase a transom latch, cupboard latch, gate latch, or doorknob from a hardware store. The latch must close automatically when the door is pushed shut

THE UNSAFE "SAFETY" GATES

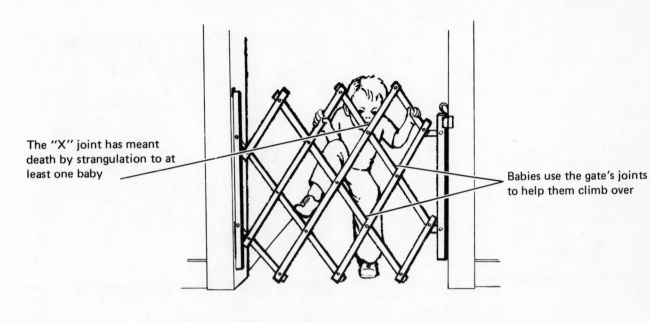

The "X" joint has meant death by strangulation to at least one baby

Babies use the gate's joints to help them climb over

All safety gates presently on the market are dangerous because they give parents a false sense of security about staircases and other household hazards

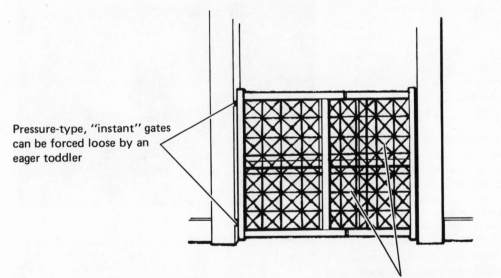

Pressure-type, "instant" gates can be forced loose by an eager toddler

Baby can get a toe hold in the wide plastic mesh and vault himself over the top

and should only open when the handle is turned. (Magnetic or spring latches are unsuitable.)

3. Install the second latch 5½ to 6' above floor level. If you are using a kitchen cupboard, try to place the two latches at least 40" apart.

Many safety experts suggest that barriers are needed at both the top and the bottom of staircases to protect your baby from falls. One suggestion is to construct removable plywood gates that, rather than swinging on hinges, slide up and down in wooden grooves screwed firmly into either side of the wall. These gates must be raised and replaced by an adult and cannot be lifted by a child.

So-called safety gates now on the market are far from safe. The accordion-style gate offers a toe hold for climbing, and some children have strangled from falling into the "X" joints of the gate. Pressure gates, which rely on the friction of rubber knobs against the side of the wall, have also been proven unsafe. They simply are not strong enough to contain eager toddlers. It's much more dangerous for a baby to fall down the stairs along with the gate than just by himself.

Some parents have found it helpful to child-proof Baby's room completely and then to install a screen door in addition to the room's entry door. The screen can be latched from the outside of the room. Mother can always see Baby and vice versa.

SAFETY TRAINING FOR OLDER BABIES

It is important that you begin working with your baby as early as possible to help him learn the skills necessary for safety. For example: When your toddler learns to climb, begin daily games of crawling up and backing down stairs. Offer ample encouragement, and take him away from the stairs at the first sign of any resistance to the experience.

When bathing him, fill the bathtub so that the water is at Baby's chest level when he's seated, and then let him practice changing from a crawling to a sitting position and back in the water. Since water movement and land movement are not the same, this is a difficult skill that will require him to arch his neck and move his feet from behind him to under him. It may very well save his life if he should fall in shallow water. Otherwise be sure to bathe Baby in very shallow water, and never leave him in the tub by himself. (A detailed discussion of bathing is on p. 14.)

Another first lesson about safety is the meaning of the word *hot*. It would be wise to let Baby go ahead and touch a hot stove. Repeat the word *hot* over and over again: "*Hot!* The stove's *hot!*" Thereafter, most babies will develop a healthy respect for the word *hot*, even when it is applied to other things such as fires and food.

SAFETY PRODUCTS

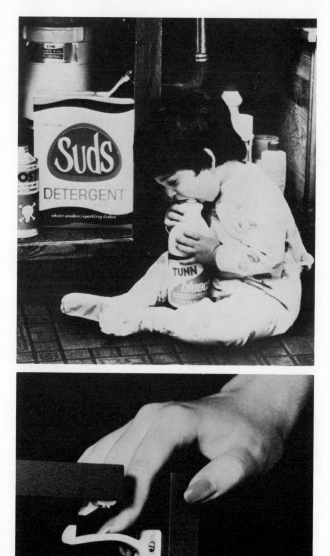

Child Safety Latch

The Kindergard Child Safety Latch is made of flexible molded nylon. It consists of a long, slender hook and a catch, which can be installed on drawers and cabinets to prevent toddlers from getting into them. The latch can only be released by an adult pressing down through a small opening in the door permitted by the latch. Available in many stores, or order from: *Kindergard Corp., 14822 Venture Dr., Dallas, TX 75234 (3 for $3.00, or 7 for $5.00)*

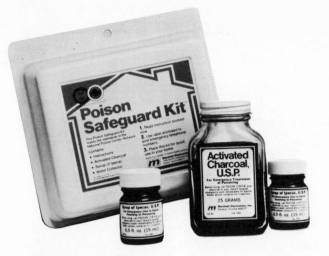

Poison Safeguard Kit

The packet includes activated charcoal to drink in solution, as directed, to counteract certain poisons; syrup of Ipecac to induce vomiting, as directed by a physician or poison control center; a specimen collector; labels for emergency telephone numbers; and an instruction brochure. Order from:
F & H Baby Products, P.O. Box 2228, Evansville, IN 47714 ($10.50 postpaid)

Safety Medicine Cabinet

This cabinet can be opened only by an adult applying pressure at the top. The angled top comes down to make a shelf for dispensing medicines while the cabinet is open. (Note: The bathroom is a poor place for medicine storage because of its humidity.)
Mothercare-by-Mail, 196 Quaker Bridge Mall, U.S. Rt. 1 and Quaker Bridge Rd., Lawrenceville, NJ 08648 (Approx. $32.50)

Corner Guard

Made of soft, nontoxic rubber, this pad for table corners applies with nondamaging adhesive tabs. Comes in a dark color to blend with furniture. Order from:
F & H Baby Products, P.O. Box 2228, Evansville, IN 47714 (6 for $4.50)

Edge Guard

The self-adhering backing makes these press-on strip guards suitable for protecting babies from falls into window sills, fireplaces, coffee tables, counter tops, bed frames and other sharp objects. Comes in a package of three 18-inch strips in black and brown. Order from:
F & H Baby Products, P.O. Box 2228, Evansville, IN 47714 ($5.25 per package)

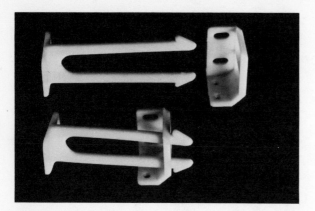

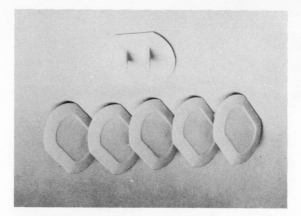

Safety Door Latch

A simple two-pronged device that keeps small children out of cabinets and drawers where dangerous articles are stored. Made of molded nylon and available in drug and variety stores. Manufactured by: *Reliance Products Corp., 108 Mason St., Woonsocket, RI 02895 (2 for under $2.00)*

Wall Plug Protectors

These Reliance outlet covers plug right in to keep out curious tots. Similar designs are available at most hardware stores or can be ordered from: *F & H Baby Products, Box 2228, Evansville, IN 47714 (20 for $1.50)*

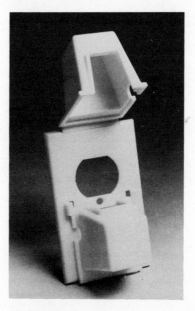

Cabinet Lock

Designed to keep small children out of the medicine cabinet, this lock opens by the touch of a button from the top of the cabinet, where youngsters can't reach. Easy-mount double-stick adhesive holds the device in place. Available in variety and drug stores. Manufactured by: *Reliance Products Corp., 108 Mason St., Woonsocket, RI 02895 (Approx. $1.50)*

Outlet Cover

With this cover, appliances and lights can be kept plugged in while safely protected from small children's probing. The outlet cover must be squeezed to open. Available in drug and variety stores. Manufactured by: *Reliance Products Corp., 108 Mason St., Woonsocket, RI 02895 (Approx. $1.50)*

SAFETY HARNESSES

A harness is an excellent safety purchase for parents of beginning crawlers and older tots. It's handiest for outdoor and shopping-center adventuring with a new, unsteady walker. Babies and mothers are both happier when Baby is allowed freedom to roam and yet can be given a little restraint from curbs, holes, and other potential dangers. The harness should always be used in strollers and highchairs that do not have both a crotch strap and a seat belt (see the chapter on chairs, pp. 44–51).

Echo Baby-Com

A small intercom system, this unit operates in conjunction with any AM radio. The radio must be within a 300-foot range of the small transmitter. The unit can be tuned in to any unused frequency between 1200 and 1650 kHz. Each unit comes with a 3-meter antenna wire and an AC power supply. Manufactured by: *Fanon/Courier Corp., 990 South Fair Oaks Ave., Pasadena, CA 91105 (Approx. $16.50)*

Mothercare Harness

Imported from England, this harness has a stainless steel back clasp that Baby can't undo. The waist and shoulder straps are independently adjustable. For use in highchairs, strollers, grocery carts, and with tottery walking babies. Write for a catalogue: *Mothercare-by-Mail, 196 Quaker Bridge Mall, U.S. Rt. 1 and Quaker Bridge Rd., Lawrenceville, NJ 08648 (Approx. $6.50)*

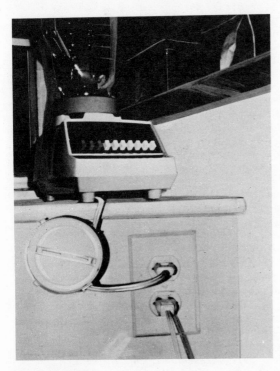

Cord A Way

These functional plastic cassettes hold appliance wires up out of Baby's reach to prevent accidents. Available in brown or white. Order from: *F & H Baby Products, Box 2228, Evansville, IN 47714 (3 for $5.25)*

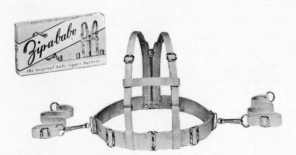

Zip-A-Babe Harness

A completely adjustable harness made of fabric webbing. The shoulder straps, the waist, and the length of the walking reins can all be adjusted for comfortable fit. It quickly zips and unzips in the back for easy use and can be carried in pocket or purse. It comes in pink, blue, or yellow, and can be found in many children's clothing stores. Order from:
Life Manufacturing Co., Inc., 20 Meridian St., E. Boston, MA 02128 ($3.00 + 50¢ shipping and handling)

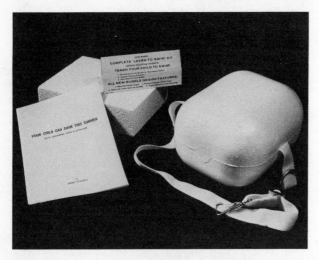

Swim-Aid

A polystyrene foam bubble on a belt to use as a floating aid for tots eighteen months and older learning simple swimming skills. The belt has a child-proof catch that is fastened around the child's waist. The Learn-to-Swim Kit includes instructions for teaching, the bubble, and extra foam for a smaller bubble to use when your child gains proficiency. Order from:
Mrs. Janet Rogers, P.O. Box 933, Dunedin, FL 33528 ($5.00 a kit)

BOOKS AND BROCHURES ON SAFETY AND POISONING

Many poison control centers have free educational materials and "Mr. Yuk" stickers to warn toddlers about poisonous substances.

The A-B-C's of Child Safety

Channing L. Bete Co., Greenfield, MA 01301 (25¢)
A delightful, easy-to-read brochure with clear illustrations of safety hazards and suggestions. Easily understood safety concepts are divided according to age levels of babies, beginning with the "wiggle-roll-put-it-in-your-mouth era." Excellent guide for your baby sitter.

The Children's Hospital Accident Handbook

Department of Health Education, The Children's Hospital Medical Center, 300 Longwood Ave., Boston, MA 02115 (35¢)
A first-aid brochure for parents: what to do for bleeding, burns, cuts, choking, head injuries, poisoning, and shock. You'll refer to it again and again — so put it in a handy place in your home.

Home Child Safety Program Kit

National Safety Council, 425 N. Michigan Avenue, Chicago, IL 60611 ($1.58)
Publicity materials, resource information, and educational materials all gathered together in one folder for parents who are concerned about infant and child safety and would like to do something about it in their own communities.

A Medical Emergency Guide: Panic or Plan?

Metropolitan Life Insurance Co., 1 Madison Ave., NYC 10010 (Free)
Test your medical emergency I.Q. with this handy guide to emergency care in home injuries. Includes a home safety list and suggestions for safety on the road.

A Sigh of Relief: The First-Aid Handbook for Childhood Emergencies

Martin I. Green
Bantam Books, 666 Fifth Ave., NYC 10019 ($7.95, paperback)
A handy book that can be an immediate reference aid in case of accidents or poisoning. Clear, large illustrations guide you through the basics of first-aid and safety.

Young Children and Accidents in the Home

U.S. Department of Health, Education and Welfare
Order from: Superintendent of Documents, U.S. Government Printing Office, Washington, DC 20402 (65¢)
A brochure for quick reference dealing with all aspects of infant and toddler safety. Included is a wall chart to instruct you in the care of cuts, burns, sprains, and other injuries.

Your Child and Household Safety

Dr. Jay M. Arena
Chemical Specialties Manufacturer's Assoc., Suite 1120,
1001 Connecticut Ave., N.W., Washington, DC 20036
(50¢)
The most compact and helpful of all the safety literature listed here! This fifteen-page brochure advises
parents of safety precautions to take at each stage of a
baby's and toddler's growth. It also suggests appropriate toys for each stage and gives an outline of emergency first-aid measures.

Your Child's Safety

Metropolitan Life Insurance Co., 1 Madison Ave., NYC
10010 (Free)
Helpful hints on protecting the very young and the
growing child. Includes suggestions for play materials
and ways you can prepare now for future emergencies.

Note: Not all manufacturers and publishers will
accept single orders for a product or book. Always
write them first, before sending money, to be certain that they will accept your order and make
sure that you have the most recent price, including shipping and handling charges.

Shoes and Booties

Babies have *naturally* flat feet. Arches don't develop until much later. The best treatment for a baby's feet is to let her go barefoot as much as possible. Her feet are normally colder than the rest of her body, so don't feel that they must always be covered. She needs the sensitivity of her feet as she begins to walk and her feet's natural nonslip treads to negotiate the climbs and risky changes in direction that are such an important part of toddler learning.

You may find that Baby gets a kind of toe burn when crawling on carpets. Outdoors, too, may present hazards to the crawler and walker — broken glass and rough asphalt are particularly dangerous for feet and toes. In these cases, the wisest choice would be a leather or cloth moccasin, or a flexible tennis shoe.

Don't let a zealous salesclerk convince you that babies must have stiff-soled, high-topped boots with artificial arches for proper foot development. Studies in foot health have found just the opposite — feet that are allowed to grow naturally with no hindrance from shoes are healthier and better aligned. An interesting study recently published in a pediatric journal reported that of 279 pediatricians, three-fourths felt that tennis shoes were perfectly adequate for babies' feet.

Here are the features to look for when purchasing infant and toddler shoes:
- Proper fit: Always try the shoes on the baby before buying them.
- The shoe should be completely flexible.
- The soles should have a tread or at least a non-slippery finish.
- The sides of the shoe should fit below the ankle bone so that there is no rubbing.
- Toes should always be covered to prevent stubbing and to keep sticks and rocks from getting caught in the shoe.
- Zippers and buckles are preferred over laces for closings, since toddlers are likely to untie laces at the first opportunity, or to trip over them.
- Feel the inside of the shoe with your fingers — are there any rough edges that could rub and cause blisters and discomfort? (Later, examine Baby's feet every time you take her shoes off to see that there are no red areas from rubbing.)

SHOE AND BOOTIE RECOMMENDATIONS

Leather Booties
Kitten-soft booties made of glove leather (#7443B) in saddle for a small baby and crawler. Two sizes: 2 (up to six months) and 3 (six to ten months). Order from: *Casco Bay Trading Post, Freeport, ME 04032 ($6.95 a pair)*

Griffin Scuffers

Scuffers have been loved by little Californians for over thirty years! They're a soft, pliable leather shoe with a side-buckling T-strap. The flat, flexible soles offer little resistance to a new walker. Available in several styles. Colors: red, white, or tan. For leaflet, or to order (send outline of baby's feet), write:
Griffin Shoe Co., 373 4th St., Oakland, CA 94607 ($7.00 + $1.25 postage and handling)

Mothercare T-Bar Play Shoes

This soft-topped, blue-and-white-checked fabric play shoe for toddlers has a side buckle, slip-resistant soles, and a rubber toe guard. For a free catalogue of their excellent infant products write:
Mothercare-by-Mail, 196 Quaker Bridge Mall, U.S. Rt. 1 and Quaker Bridge Rd., Lawrenceville, NJ 08648 (Approx. $6.00 a pair)

Note: Not all manufacturers and publishers will accept single orders for a product or book. Always write them first, before sending money, to be certain that they will accept your order and make sure that you have the most recent price, including shipping and handling charges.

Strollers, Sleds, and Accessories

In the past few years, the lightweight-stroller industry has blossomed, giving us a huge variety of easy-to-store strollers to select from. Many parents I have spoken with feel the "umbrella" stroller has been one of their best investments, because of its convenience for walks and in shopping centers. Other parents have found this purchase to be a real lemon. The aluminum frame bends and snaps in two, the footrest tears apart, the upholstery stretches and rips, or the front wheels fall off. It looks as if the designers of these strollers have sacrificed durability for portability. One mother wailed, "I just wish it would last through *one* baby!"

Lightweight strollers don't fare very well from a design standpoint either. The seats are too deep for an average baby under two, the footrests seldom can be used by a baby for support, and the strollers are very unstable, tipping over backward with the brush of a feather. The sling-like seats of many models throw babies and tots into an uncomfortable forward slump, with shoulders rounded.

Some parents purchase middle-weight strollers because these heavier models offer better postural support, easier steering, better durability, and a place to store packages while shopping. The bigger strollers have their drawbacks, however. Above all, they are very awkward to set up and collapse. Parents have also reported frequent tears in the vinyl upholstery on models that suspend the seat with a crotch strap that snaps to the front bars. The reclining seat does seem to offer a good compromise between a carriage and an upright stroller, but there is danger to Baby if the sides of the stroller are unprotected, permitting him to roll out.

There is another alternative, however. The best solution seems to be a really good, though expensive, lightweight stroller that has a padded reclining seat, a wider wheel base for stability, and the durability of chromed steel. The best designs on the market, more often than not, are imported strollers. American manufacturers have yet to exhibit the care in materials and design shown by the Italian Perego models (imported by Barclay Co., P.O. Box 37, Teaneck, NJ 07666, and sold by Sears), the Italian Vai models (imported by Collier-Keyworth Co., Gardner, MA 01440), and the English Silver Cross models (imported by Simmons Juvenile Products, 613 E. Beacon Ave., New London, WI 54961).

All of these imported strollers have well-padded upholstery, reclining seat backs, good brakes, and a superb durability record. They are also quite expensive, as lightweight strollers go, costing between $50.00 and $120.00. Is the durability and comfort to Baby worth the expense? The answer lies in your own needs. Will you be taking long walks? Do you usually shop in centers that require much walking? Do you plan to be in airports frequently? If so, an initial investment in a good, durable stroller is wise, rather than wasting time and money on a cheap stroller that may not hold up even through the first year.

My suggestion is to make a money tradeoff. Buy the best lightweight stroller and the best car seat you can afford and plan to skip all the unnecessary doodads of Baby's first year. Just by using cloth rather than paper diapers, you can almost make up the difference. By skipping a walker, a jumper, unneeded baby clothes, and a dressing table, you can afford the durability and comfort you need in the products you are apt to use the most during your child's first three years.

Whether you find a good, imported stroller or opt for a top-of-the-line American stroller, here are some important guidelines you should follow when shopping:

• Collapse and open a stroller several times to make

sure that doing so is a simple and convenient maneuver. Strollers that can be operated by one hand are better than those requiring both hands, since they allow you to hold Baby at the same time.

• Choose a model with a reclining back so that your younger baby can rest comfortably, as well as your napping tot later on.

• Test the equilibrium of the stroller by pressing downward on the handles. The stroller should have adequate resistance to tipping over backward.

• Try steering the stroller first with one hand and then the other, to see if it will stay on a straight course. If the stroller veers, you can be sure that you'll have a difficult journey when trying to carry packages and push Baby at the same time.

• Check for some form of shock absorption. The stroller should either have rubber inserts in the rear or front, to prevent jarring, or it should have rubber tires. Avoid strollers with rigid plastic tires.

• Test the brake. The best brakes are those that come on both rear wheels and offer positive locking, such as those that press between two spokes on the wheel so that the wheel cannot move.

• Look for external hazards that might hurt a falling or playing baby. There should be no protruding bolts on the wheel mounts and no danger of pinching or crushing from joints or from collapsing or opening the stroller.

• Examine the restraining belts to make sure that they cannot be loosened by a squirming baby and that they are easy to operate.

• Give vinyls the "pinch" test to see if they are thick enough to withstand wear at pressure points, such as the corners where the seat joins the frame.

A POORLY DESIGNED STROLLER

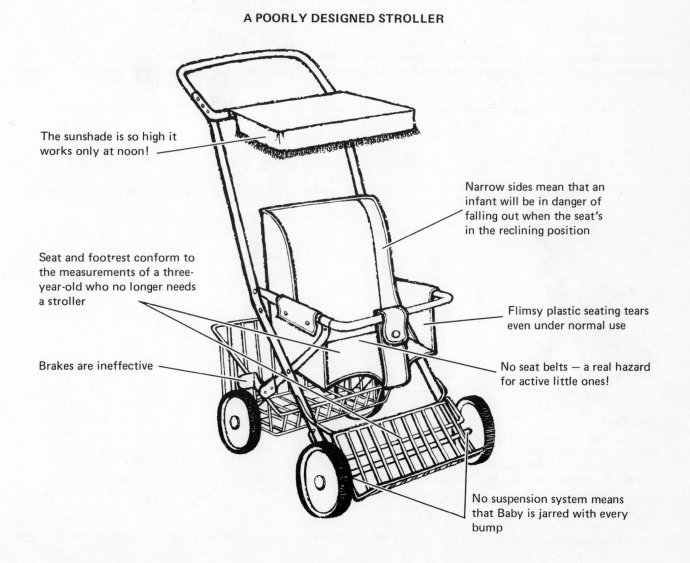

The sunshade is so high it works only at noon!

Narrow sides mean that an infant will be in danger of falling out when the seat's in the reclining position

Seat and footrest conform to the measurements of a three-year-old who no longer needs a stroller

Flimsy plastic seating tears even under normal use

Brakes are ineffective

No seat belts — a real hazard for active little ones!

No suspension system means that Baby is jarred with every bump

STROLLERS AND ACCESSORIES

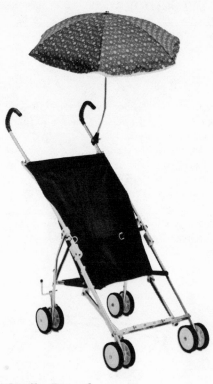

The Perego Stroller

Imported from Italy, this well-designed medium-weight stroller has a four-wheel suspension system. Its two-wheel brakes are easily engaged by foot from the rear. It also features high padded sides, an adjustable back and footrest, and a safety belt plus a crotch belt. Can be collapsed for storage. (Model shown: Elba L5 with optional shopping basket.) Distributed by: *Barclay Co., P.O. Box 37, Teaneck, NJ 07666* *(Approx. $70.00)*

Stroller Parasol

A small umbrella that fits on the arm of strollers, carriages or swings, it is adjustable for providing shade anywhere. (Stroller shown is the O. K. Baby Stroller and is also available by mail from Mothercare.) *Mothercare-by-Mail, 196 Quaker Bridge Mall, U.S. Rt. 1 and Quaker Bridge Rd., Lawrenceville, NJ 08648* *(Parasol, approx. $11.00; stroller, approx. $35.00)*

Cosy Toes

A roomy, two-legged bag with furlike fabric lining, made especially for stroller passengers. Adjustable straps hold the Cosy Toes up. Perfect for taking Baby out on cold winter days! Ask for their free catalogue of baby clothing and products: *Mothercare-by-Mail, 196 Quaker Bridge Mall, U.S. Rt. 1 and Quaker Bridge Rd., Lawrenceville, NJ 08648* *(Under $20.00)*

SLEDS AND ACCESSORIES

Baby Sled

A wooden baby sled (Model No. 800) with wheels that can be lowered for bare ground. The handle can be used to push the sled or reversed for pulling it. It can be converted into a regular sled later. An optional cushioned vinyl seat pad (No. 805) with a pocket for Baby's feet can be tied onto the sled. Order from:
Paris Mfg. Corp., P.O. Box 250, S. Paris, ME 04281 ($35.95 + shipping — 15 lbs.; with pad, $46.90)

Sno-Jet Baby Boggan

A small toboggan made of contoured plastic for a baby. It has a raised seat and a safety strap. The handle can be attached in the front or rear. For more information, write:
Coléco Industries, Inc., 945 Asylum Ave., Hartford, CT 06105 (Under $20.00)

Toys

Let's set the record straight: you are your baby's first and foremost toy. Or, to put it another way, a baby needs people, not objects. It is with you that she will learn about the world — whether it can be trusted, if it's a good place to be, if it brings warmth and happy feelings. It is with you that she explores sights, smells, and textures. And you are the one she needs close by to carry her, talk to her, caress her, and love her. No toy will buy off a baby's compelling need for personal contact.

Toys for babies and children are tremendously overrated in our affluent society. Advertisers bombard children's television programs and parents' magazines to promote the idea that toys are a part of the joy of life. Little children are shown saying, "I love you!" over and over to toys. Each child is expected to have an abundance of toys along with food to eat and shoes to wear. Parents invest over four billion dollars a year in toys for Christmas, birthdays, and the like, with the mistaken belief that they are showering love on their little ones. The backlash of this excessive valuing of toys is the 700,000 children a year who are sickened, injured, maimed, or even killed by them.

Toys never seem half as pleasing or entertaining to Baby as parents and grandparents expect them to be. We buy toys on the assumption that Baby will be overjoyed with them and play contentedly with her newly discovered objects for hours. Often she's more interested in the box or the wrapping paper than in the toy. It's just not in a baby's nature to be satisfied by or involved with one object for more than a few moments at a time. As they become creepers and walkers, babies cruise around continuously looking for some new feat, some intricacy to finger, or new particles to mouth. The marvels of our toy-making industry have to compete with T.V. knobs, the dirt in the potted plants, the ash-tray on the coffee table, and the hole in the upholstery.

This is not to say that toys can't play a role in a baby's development. A truly well-chosen toy that fits a particular interest of Baby's at the right point in her development can help to satisfy her inner drives to explore and learn. Here are some important points to look for when evaluating a toy for a baby:

• It should be free of sharp edges or points, including corners. An infant is continually falling as she masters getting from one place to another. Any sharp object in the path of her fall can be hazardous.

• It should have no exposed mechanical parts that might catch small fingers.

• It should not be run by batteries, which may leak acid and cause disfiguring burns when an infant tries to mouth the toy.

• It should have no small or removable parts that a baby could put in her mouth. The danger is that Baby might inhale them, blocking her windpipe and causing death by suffocation. (Suffocation from an ingested object takes the lives of nine hundred babies and children under five every year.) Be particularly careful about buttons and button eyes on stuffed toys.

• It should be unbreakable. Avoid brittle plastics, which break into sharp splinters. Also avoid rough woods, which splinter, and glass objects, including glass hand mirrors.

• It should be safe for chewing and washable. Avoid dolls and stuffed animals if the hair fibers can be pulled off. Avoid painted toys unless they are clearly labeled *non-toxic*, which means that the paint is free from poisonous lead.

• Avoid balloons. They have caused numerous suffocation deaths by becoming entrapped in the throats of infants and young children, even though they were inflated only moments earlier.

UNSAFE TOYS

A cheap rattle breaks easily, exposing sharp edges that can cut and pellets that can become lodged in the windpipe, causing suffocation

Ears have sharp, piercing wire ribs

This stuffed toy is highly flammable and could be easily set afire by a careless cigarette

Eyes can be pulled off to expose sharp metal sprockets. Babies have suffocated by choking on button eyes

Hair comes off by the handful and is eaten by babies

BEWARE THE SHARP EDGES

Sharp points and edges are always dangerous because babies frequently fall on them

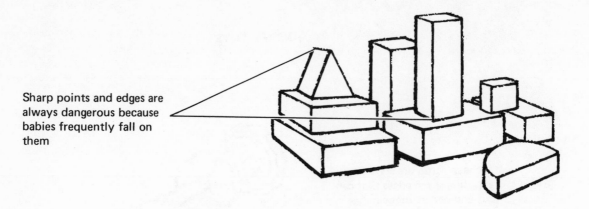

When left in the crib these sharp edges have caused abrasions of the eye in babies

Beware wheels that can be removed to expose a sharp metal rod and parts that can pinch

• Small rattles, which are often tied on packages at baby showers, should be discarded. They come in the shape of diaper pins and telephone receivers. Five babies have died from them, so the U.S. Consumer Product Safety Commission has banned them from the market, though many may still be in circulation. Babies get these rattles jammed in their throats, causing strangulation.

• Select the right toy for Baby's stage in development. For example, a ride-on toy is an excellent choice for a secure walker, but a hazard to a newly walking baby who is unable to lift her leg to mount it without falling into the toy.

• Toys that have lasting value over many stages of interest in a baby's and young child's growth are the best purchases. An example is a wooden cart that could first be used as a walker and later as a baby carriage or wagon for an older tot.

A creative way of dealing with Baby's natural restlessness and need for experiences is to use your own resources. Why buy an expensive music-box mobile that comes with warnings that it cannot be touched or chewed, when you can make your own colorful mobile from things around the house? (Be sure to get a copy of Nova University's *Plan and Learn Program*, mentioned at the end of the chapter, for many do-it-yourself ideas.) It's fun to experiment with Baby's unfolding world and to discover what intrigues her and turns her on. Batting on a white paper bag may be just what your two-month-old loves; jangling a set of measuring spoons could mean great joy to your six-month-old; spinning pots around might please your one-year-old. Keep a "Let's see how you like this!" attitude, and you both can have fun together.

AN UNSAFE SWING

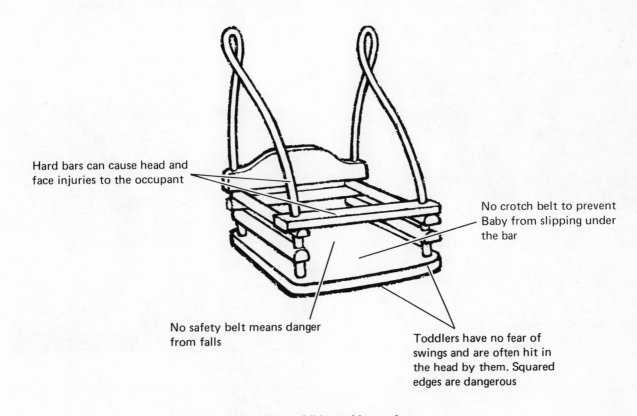

Hard bars can cause head and face injuries to the occupant

No crotch belt to prevent Baby from slipping under the bar

No safety belt means danger from falls

Toddlers have no fear of swings and are often hit in the head by them. Squared edges are dangerous

Never let a child stand in a swing

FOR NEW BABIES
(Birth to Two Months of Age)

Homemade mobile to go over the dressing table or crib
Brightly patterned bed sheets
A soft fur pelt to lie on

FOR BABIES WHO CAN HOLD THINGS AND THOSE BEGINNING TO SIT UP
(Three to Five Months)

A note on teethers: the two best teethers are a cold carrot stick (before Baby is able to bite off chunks) and a cold terry washcloth that's been wrung out.

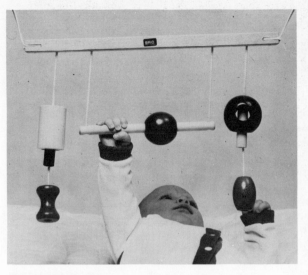

Wooden Crib Gym

Bright yellow, green, red, and blue are the colors of this intriguing crib plaything. Made in Sweden, it can be tied across the crib or play space for a baby's earliest touching, pulling, grabbing, and kicking. Order from the catalogue of:
Children's Design Center, 29 Excelsior Springs Ave., Saratoga Springs, NY 12866
($15.00 + $1.50 postage and handling)

Animal Grabbers

These safe, soft terry animals are foam-filled. A blue elephant, a yellow flop-eared dog, and a pink pig are available. Each has been carefully constructed for baby use, with lock-stitching for durability. Each is machine washable and safe for the dryer. Their circular shape means easy grasping for Baby. Available in toy departments. Manufactured by:
Fisher-Price Toys, East Aurora, NY 14052
(Approx. $3.75 ea.)

Musical Kicking Toy

Even very young babies enjoy kicking this colorful foam-filled fabric block, which has jingle bells safely imbedded inside. The toy fastens to the crib bars or playpen sides by elasticized ribbon. Order from:
Barbistuff, 635 Tualiitan Rd., Los Angeles, CA 90049
($8.98)

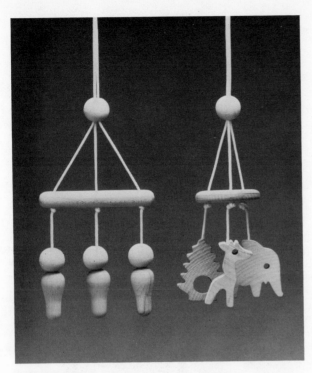

Crib Exercisers

Clackety wooden figures for Baby's hands and feet. The people-shaped crib exerciser is made of wooden pieces suspended from sturdy cords. The animal exerciser has a wooden elephant, a giraffe, and a tree. Order from:
Nursery Originals, Inc., 280 Rand St., Central Falls, RI 02863 ($4.50 + $1.25 postage and handling)

FOR BABIES WHO CAN SIT WELL
(Six to Nine Months)

Johnson & Johnson Playpath Series

The rattle has a red ball inside that circles around and around before disappearing into the handle. This and other well-designed baby toys — a folding display box with a mirror on it, a line of teddy bears to fasten onto the crib, and a suctioned table-top toy, for example — are mailed to parents who subscribe to the Playpath program. Each toy is accompanied by a detailed brochure explaining how to use it effectively. Subscribers receive toys every 45 days. The cost of the toys is approximately $9.95 per mailing. There is a return policy and cancellation clause. For a brochure describing the program, write:
Johnson & Johnson Baby Products, 6 Commercial St., Hicksville, NY 11801

Clutch Ball *(left)*

Bright checks and solid colors make this ball a special joy, as does the shape, which allows small fingers to grasp it. The ball is approximately 7 inches in diameter. Order from the catalogue of:
Children's Design Center, 29 Excelsior Springs Ave., Saratoga Springs, NY 12866 ($9.00 + $1.25 postage)

Cuddly Doll

A completely handmade 9" baby doll stuffed with non-allergenic polyester fiberfill. It has embroidered features and a soft fabric body. Order from this working community of mentally handicapped adults, specifying white or black and girl, boy, or baby that appears to be either sex. (Free brochure describing other handmade items mailed upon request.)
Camphill Village Gift Shop, Chrysler Pond Rd., Copake, NY 12516 ($6.00 plus postage)

Tupperware Shape-O

A hollow plastic ball of bright red and blue containing a variety of plastic shapes that can be fitted into the proper holes. Use as a ball now and later (at eighteen to twenty-four months of age) for sorting shapes. Look for local Tupperware distributors in your telephone directory, or write for information to:
Tupperware Home Parties, Orlando, FL 32802 ($4.89)

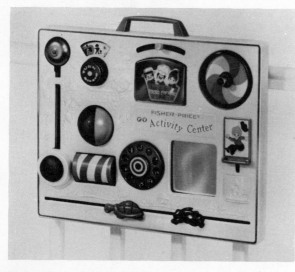

Fisher-Price Activity Center

A very well designed toy for developing finger and hand coordination. Knobs turn; balls twirl; squeakers, bells, and rattles can be set into motion. (Don't confuse the Fisher-Price Center with other, poorly designed boxes that have sharp edges and lack the variety of colors.) Most large toy departments carry it, or for "where to find it" information, write:
Fisher-Price Toys, 606 Girard Ave., E. Aurora, NY 14052 (Approx. $11.25)

Wooden Rattle

Imported from Sweden, this bright red and yellow Brio rattle is 5½ inches long. Just the right size for babies to grip. Order from the catalogue of:
Children's Design Center, 29 Excelsior Springs Ave., Saratoga Springs, NY 12866
($10.00 + $1.25 postage and handling)

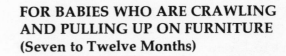

FOR BABIES WHO ARE CRAWLING AND PULLING UP ON FURNITURE
(Seven to Twelve Months)

A Baby Walker Wagon

Baby loves being able to push a large object in front of her as she is beginning to pull up and walk. A square, smooth-edged plastic laundry basket turned upside-down becomes a fine push-me object; a wheeled hassock that has nice padding will also be fun for Baby. Creative Playthings has discontinued making a walker on casters with a rubber bumper in the front, to prevent scratches to furniture, and a chrome push handle, but you may still be able to find one at a yard sale.

Suctioned Rattle

The Whirly 3 sits on the highchair tray or adheres to the side of the bathtub for play. It is constructed of red, green, and yellow plastic, with bright yellow rattle shapes inside the clear upper domes. The flexible base allows the rattles to knock against one another. Order from the catalogue of:
Mothercare-by-Mail, 196 Quaker Bridge Mall, U.S. Rt. 1 and Quaker Bridge Rd., Lawrenceville, NJ 08648 (Approx. $5.50)

Wooden Carry Wagon (*above*)

A stabilizer for new walkers as well as a plaything for a child, this wagon is an excellent investment for the preschool years. The blue handle is 19½" high. Order from the catalogue of:
Children's Design Center, 29 Excelsior Springs Ave., Saratoga Springs, NY 12866 ($27.50 + $2.00 postage and handling)

Wooden Car (*left*)

The Roll and Play hand car is 7½" long and made entirely of smooth wood. It is so safe and strong, Baby can chew on it, roll it on the floor and even up the wall. Can be found in specialty shops, or ordered from:
Bill Muller Wooden Toys, Rockhill Industrial Park, 87 Commerce Dr., Telford, PA 18969 ($4.00)

FOR EXPERIENCED WALKERS AND CLIMBERS
(Twelve to Twenty-four Months)

A "Drag" Doll

Walking babies love having a dolly that they can carry around with them. The Camphill doll is hand-sewn with bright fabrics and stuffed with nonallergenic fiberfill. A special feature of the dolly is its long string hair, which little ones like to use as a handle for dragging the doll about. Specify black or white, boy or girl. *Camphill Village Gift Shop, Chrysler Pond Rd., Copake, NY 12516 ($8.00 plus postage)*

Mini Wheels

A wheeled toy for beginners — eighteen months to three years (up to 45 lbs. and 30" to 38" tall) — that is low to the ground and has wide-track rear wheels so that it will not tip over easily. Made of molded plastic in bright red and blue, it's not as durable as a tricycle but much safer and easier to mount. For "where to find it" information, write: *Louis Marx Co., 45 Church St., Stamford, CT 06906 (Under $20.00)*

Rocking Horse Pattern

Just trace the pattern on wood and saw it out for an inexpensive rocking horse or elephant. The directions for decorating and painting come too. Order pattern #56 (for both horse and elephant) from: *U-Bild Enterprises, Box 2383, Van Nuys, CA 91409 ($2.00)*

Floating Family

The modern equivalent to a rubber duckie — this boat, pitcher, and turtle have three floating friends for bathtub voyages. They're made of brightly colored, unbreakable plastic. Manufactured by: *Fisher-Price Toys, 606 Girard Ave., East Aurora, NY 14052 (Approx. $8.00 a set)*

Activity Chair

This chair is constructed of wood and is available in bright red or yellow with white sides. It can be used as a chair, as a stepping stool for the bathroom, or as a floor activity desk for projects. Assembly is required. Order from:
Nursery Originals, Inc., 280 Rand St., Central Falls, RI 02863 ($18.00 plus $4.00 shipping)

Wooden Doll Carriage

A sturdy wooden push toy made by the Society of Brothers, a small religious community. This carriage (Model D-12) is heavy enough so that most new walkers can push it without any fear of its tipping backwards. It sports bright red wheels with rubber rims and is strong enough for a little one to ride in, too. Also write for their catalogue of well-designed toys:
Community Playthings, Rifton, NY 12471 ($32.50 + approx. $4.00 shipping and handling)

Birch Rocker (Model #856)

A sturdy wooden rocker that can withstand toddler abuse. This chair features rounded edges at base, arms, seat, and back. Although it comes without a cushion, added padding would probably make it more comfortable. Manufactured by:
Hedstrom Co., Bedford, PA 15522 (Approx. $39.00)

Indoor Gym House

Of all the investments you make in play equipment, this one will probably give you the most for your money. From early climbing tots to energetic pre-schoolers, this slide will have a long, active life indoors or out. Sturdy wood construction with a crawl-in hiding place. (Cat. #85A102) Order from:
Kaplan Corp., P.O. Box 15027, Winston-Salem, NC 27103 ($46.50 + $6.60 shipping and handling)

You can make your own gym house with a pattern from:
U-Bild Enterprises, Box 2383, Van Nuys, CA 91409 (#580 Indoor Slide Pattern, $1.50)

BOOKS AND BROCHURES

MAKING TOYS FOR BABIES

Easy-to-Do Toys and Activities for Infants and Toddlers

Beverly Upchurch
Infant Care Project, Institute for Child and Family Development, The University of North Carolina at Greensboro, Greensboro, NC 27412 ($1.00)
Ideas for making mobiles, rattles, a stick horse, and other baby toys, along with suggestions for records and songs for little ones.

Fun in the Making

Children's Bureau, U.S. Department of Health, Education and Welfare
Order from: Superintendent of Documents, U.S. Government Printing Office, Washington, DC 20402 (55¢)
A thirty-page pamphlet with numerous do-it-yourself ideas for toddler toys, including a rolling pull-toy made from an oatmeal box, a clattering pull-toy from spools, and a bouncy mobile from a paper plate.

Home-Made Baby Toys

Sara K. Swan
Houghton Mifflin Co., 2 Park St., Boston, MA 02107 ($4.95, paperback)
How to make your own mobiles, stuffed toys, fabric books, and even push toys. The toys are all grouped by age levels and are easy to construct from everyday materials.

Play and Learn Program

Marilyn M. Segal

From One to Two Years

Marilyn M. Segal
B. L. Winch & Associates, P.O. Box 1185, Torrance, CA 90505 (Approx. $2.00 each)
These marvelous paperback books offer hundreds of suggestions for activities with babies and toddlers. All of the recommended toys are easy to make from everyday materials. These books include instructions for making a squeak book, a horse puppet, a bath boat, and many other playthings. Both books are gems!

What to Do When "There's Nothing to Do"

The Boston Children's Medical Center and Elizabeth M. Gregg
Dell Publishing Co., 1 Dag Hammarskjöld Plaza, 245 E. 47th St., NYC 10017 ($1.50, paperback)
A guide to making toys from everyday things around the house. A mothering guide, too, particularly for difficult days when you don't feel like coping. The appendix lists books and records for children and ideas for a child who's "out of sorts." A good reference during Baby's first five years!

PLAY ACTIVITIES FOR BABIES

Baby Learning Through Baby Play: A Parent's Guide for the First Two Years

Baby to Parent, Parent to Baby
Ira J. Gordon
St. Martin's Press, 175 Fifth Ave., NYC 10010
(*$3.95 and $4.95, paperback, respectively*)
Both of Dr. Gordon's books are sensitive, helpful guides to baby care. *Baby Learning* offers games to play with Baby, while *Baby to Parent* is a parenting guide that suggests ways to handle Baby effectively. These make an excellent shower gift.

How to Play with Your Baby
Athina Aston
Fountain Publishing Co., 509 Madison Ave., NYC 10022
(*$3.95, paperback*)
A warmly human book that will guide you through the many months and small experiences that make up the first two years of a baby's life. The play chart at the end of the book is helpful in outlining the activities that you can share with your baby during this important age.

Loving and Learning: Interacting with Your Child from Birth to Three
N. J. McDiarmid, M. A. Peterson, J. R. Sutherland
Harcourt Brace Jovanovich, 757 Third Ave., NYC 10017
(*$8.95*)
An excellent guidebook for providing experiences for little ones. It contains Yoga exercises for very young babies, all sorts of feeling and touching games, and even simple cooking and scientific experiments for young tots. Each chapter provides a wealth of information on babies and tots at each stage of development. A good buy as a reference book!

"The Loving Touch" (Cassette Tape)
Dr. Ruth D. Rice
Cradle-Care, Inc., P.O. Box 401548, Dallas, TX 75240
(*$19.95*)
This cassette tape comes with a chart giving step-by-step instructions concerning the techniques of massaging and stroking babies. Used by over 2,000 mothers across the U.S. Maternal heartbeat sounds for calming a baby are also on the tape. A must for high-risk, premature, and C-section babies.

Note: Not all manufacturers and publishers will accept single orders for a product or book. Always write them first, before sending money, to be certain that they will accept your order and make sure that you have the most recent price, including shipping and handling charges.

Walkers and Jumpers

WALKERS

The U.S. Consumer Product Safety Commission estimates that in the fiscal year 1973 over 3700 persons in the U.S. received injuries associated with walkers serious enough to require emergency-room treatment. Most of the injuries occurred to babies under two years old and 90 per cent of these injuries were to the babies' heads. The major causes of injuries were the baby's tipping the walker over when attempting to go over rugs or pick up toys, entrapment (sometimes amputation) of the baby's fingers when the walker's dangerous "X" frame collapsed, and falling down the stairs in the walker. In some cases the walker was flimsy and poorly built; in other cases the babies were too large for the walkers. In most instances, parents had a false sense of security about the walker and assumed that their babies were safe and needed no supervision.

Walkers are sometimes used because parents believe that they help a baby to walk sooner. Actually, the baby in a walker is not walking; she is sitting and "sculling" with her legs — an entirely different leg action than walking. Studies are now beginning to show that crawling is an extremely vital activity that lays the foundation for later skills. It's important that no device impede a baby's continual crawling and creeping practice. A walker is also an expensive purchase, considering its short period of usefulness.

Keeping these built-in limitations in mind, here are some features to look for, should you decide to purchase a walker:

• The circular-framed walker is better designed than the collapsible model. It's more stable, moves more easily, and is less likely to collapse. *Never* put a baby in an "X"-framed collapsible walker unless the coils and locking devices have a protective covering.

• Inspect the seat to see that it is sturdy and will not break easily. Enclosed, adjustable seats are safer and more durable than suspended bicycle-type seats.

• Ideally, the leg area of the walker should be completely enclosed by a smooth metal or high-impact plastic drum. Babies often back into hot oven doors and sharp-edged corners, injuring their exposed legs.

• The exterior of the walker should have no sharp metal edges or protruding knobs that a baby could fall into from outside of the walker. Walkers are particular hazards because creeping and newly walking babies interpret walkers as playthings and like to push them around.

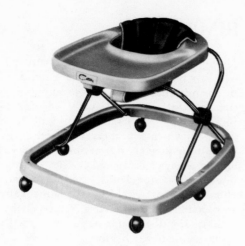

Century Super Coupe Walker

The positive features of this walker are: the height can be adjusted to your baby's needs; the wide base makes it more tip-resistant than most; the "X" joints are safely covered; and the high-back vinyl seat is superior to suspended-seat models. The six rotating casters make forward and lateral movement easy. Drawbacks are that there is no leg protection and that the seat binding is scratchy. Baby should wear long pants when using this walker. Manufactured by Century Products, Inc., Cleveland, OH 44102. Order by mail from the catalogue of:
Children's Design Center, 29 Excelsior Springs Ave., Saratoga Springs, NY 12866 ($26.00 + $2.00 shipping)

A DANGEROUS WALKER

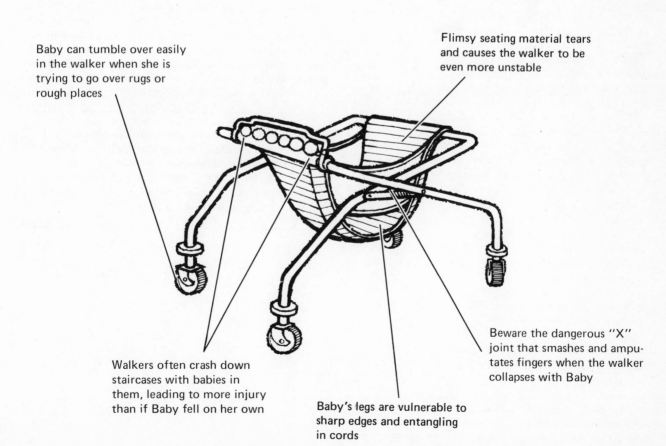

Baby can tumble over easily in the walker when she is trying to go over rugs or rough places

Flimsy seating material tears and causes the walker to be even more unstable

Walkers often crash down staircases with babies in them, leading to more injury than if Baby fell on her own

Baby's legs are vulnerable to sharp edges and entangling in cords

Beware the dangerous "X" joint that smashes and amputates fingers when the walker collapses with Baby

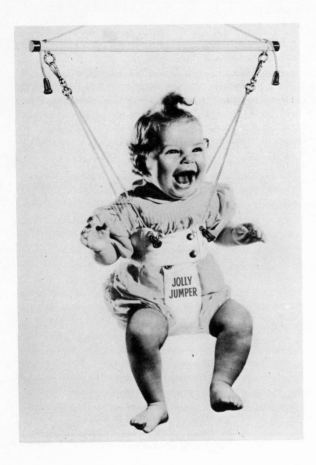

JUMPERS

A jumper is a device that allows a baby to be suspended with her toes just touching the ground. Rubber cables or springs enable the baby to move up and down by pushing with her toes. Usually the jumper is suspended in a doorway by a large clamping device. Some babies really enjoy using jumpers, while others want to get out the minute they are put in one. A baby using a jumper should always be watched closely. Mother shouldn't, as one manufacturer claims, "be free to rest, go about her chores or visit with friends, while baby is gleefully involved in healthy exercise," since a baby could hit her head on the door frame or get entrapped in the strings while trying to reach a toy.

Some specialists in infant development view the jumper as they do the walker — as a device that, if anything, impedes the baby's practice and strengthening of motor skills when used in excess. Some babies demonstrate a temporary dizziness after being taken out of the jumper, somewhat like a sailor stepping onto land after being on a ship.

Don't be afraid to try using a jumper with your baby for brief periods of time, though, if your baby seems to enjoy it. Just be sure to stay close at hand, and use a doorway that is wide enough to prevent her from hitting her head. The safest models are those that fit the baby like a waistband and have a closely fitting fabric crotch. The prices of jumpers range from $7.00 to around $14.00.

> **Note:** Not all manufacturers and publishers will accept single orders for a product or book. Always write them first, before sending money, to be certain that they will accept your order and make sure that you have the most recent price, including shipping and handling charges.

U.S. CONSUMER PRODUCT SAFETY COMMISSION
CONSUMER PRODUCT COMPLAINT FORM

If you know of an article intended for use by children or adults which you believe to present an unreasonable hazard, please let us know. The following information will enable us to take the appropriate action.

NAME OF THE ARTICLE OR A BRIEF DESCRIPTION _____
_____
_____

STOCK OR CODE NUMBERS ON ARTICLE PACKAGE _____

COUNTRY OF ORIGIN (IF IMPORTED) _____

MANUFACTURER OR IMPORTER (IF KNOWN) _____
_____

WHERE AND WHEN WAS THE ARTICLE PURCHASED? _____
_____

WHAT IS HAZARDOUS ABOUT THIS PRODUCT? _____
_____
_____
_____
_____

DO YOU KNOW OF ANY INJURIES INVOLVING THIS ITEM? ANY CLOSE CALLS? IF SO PLEASE
TELL US THE CIRCUMSTANCES. _____
_____
_____
_____
_____

YOUR NAME, ADDRESS AND TELEPHONE NUMBER _____
_____
_____

Please send this form to: U.S. Consumer Product Safety Commission
Washington, D.C. 20207

INDEX

INDEX